AF444626

THE UNINVITED: A PSYCHOLOGICAL THRILLER

NADIJA MUJAGIC

A SHARP PAIN pulses through me, seizing every nerve in its relentless grip.

"Ouch," I squeal, as Jack grips my arm harder. Sometimes he seems unaware of his own strength.

I turn to him. He's looking at something outside the window of our Uber. His eyes widen with shock.

I follow his gaze toward the stairs leading to our brownstone townhouse in Back Bay. A woman is standing there, looking around as if she's lost. I lean forward to see if I recognize her, but my memory is off, and I have no clue who she is.

We've just stepped off a red-eye from Hawaii, and I'm still a bit dazed, especially after a ten-day honeymoon.

Just as I'm about to ask Jack who the woman is, he exits

the car and heads for the stairs. But something about the way he moves feels off—stiff, almost reluctant. His shoulders are tight, and for a moment, I catch the briefest flicker of something in his eyes—fear? Guilt? I'm not sure. Whatever it is, it disappears so quickly I almost think I imagined it.

"My son!" The woman walks in Jack's direction with her arms wide open.

My mother-in-law. Evelyn Ross.

Her voice is deep and confident, instantly putting me on edge.

Jack says nothing as he walks toward her. Like me, I assume he's shocked to see his mother here. It's surprising for a few reasons: first, she lives across the country in Seattle, far from Boston, and second, she's just been through serious medical issues that should have left her immobile for a while.

Who the hell visits someone unannounced?

Jack gives his mother a tight smile, but his hands remain stiff at his sides. I can't tell if he's nervous or just tired from our flight, but something about their hug seems...off.

My phone chimes, and it's a text message from my college bestie, Jenna.

> Welcome home! Can't wait to hear how the honeymoon went.

I chuckle and look around, almost expecting Jenna to be

standing nearby. How did she know to text me just as we pull in? I don't have time to respond.

I take a closer look at my mother-in-law. Her face is caked with makeup, and she's wearing a tight skirt with her hair pulled into a bun. She looks nothing like the photos I've seen, though I can barely focus after the sleepless flight.

She's not exactly how I'd pictured her. From the stories I've heard from Jack, she'd struck me more like a frail, petite woman, not aging so gracefully. Especially with her recent health complications, which I don't know much about. But this woman—my mother-in-law—looks the opposite of that.

I shuffle down the street and head into the house, a wave of annoyance washing over me. The last thing I want is to deal with my mother-in-law, not when I've just set plans in motion for Jack. But I remind myself to be cordial and patient—after all, she's family now, and we're supposed to get along. Maybe she feels guilty for missing our wedding, though she shouldn't, given she was in the hospital, barely clinging to life.

Evelyn Ross descends the front staircase to meet me in the middle.

"Oh, look at my daughter. Emily..." Her voice is shaky, as if she's about to cry with joy.

She embraces me tightly and sniffs my hair. I look over her shoulder as we hug and see Jack standing at the door, looking at us with an unreadable face. I can't tell what he's thinking or feeling. Is he elated his mother is here?

As the shock effect wanes off, we barrage Evelyn with questions. "How long have you been waiting out here?" Jack asks as he unlocks the front door.

Evelyn rolls her eyes as if calculating the time in her mind, "Oh, I don't know. A few hours, maybe."

"A few hours!" Jack says, but his voice seems to be void of shock. It sounds fake. He must be tired. "That's a long time to wait."

"It's okay." Evelyn steps into the house and gazes around. It's obvious she's surveying the house while doing her best not to appear too snoopy. "I strolled down the street and found a cute coffee shop and had lunch. You guys live on a lively street."

Newbury Street in Boston is one of the loveliest and liveliest streets in the city. And most expensive. Adorned with many restaurants and boutique stores, Jack and I were fortunate to find an apartment and settle here. We bought it at a whooping three million, the price to pay for a prime location. Jack has always wanted to live in the hustle and bustle of the city, since he doesn't want to drive.

More precisely, he is afraid to.

The only way we can continue to afford the place is to keep working as hard as Jack and I have over the past ten years. If it wasn't for my own catering business and Jack's career as a corporate defense lawyer, we would have to kiss our dream of city life goodbye.

We walk through the hallway and the living room to the kitchen. Our place is an open concept with exceptionally high ceilings and breathtaking architecture. Evelyn hasn't stopped chit-chatting while sizing up our place, but neither Jack nor I am responding. She slides into the living room and checks the wall adorned with photos of me and Jack traveling around the world: Jack and I sailing around the Norwegian fjords; Jack and I holding hands near the Eiffel Tower; Jack and I bungee jumping in Costa Rica—all the evidence of the fun times we've had. Evelyn stops to look at the photos and studies them like they are Michelangelo's masterpieces.

For a long moment, she doesn't say anything, just stares. Her fingers hover over the glass, tracing the edge of the frame but never touching. I feel a chill in the air, though the house is warm.

"You two look so... happy here." Her voice is low, almost distant. She tilts her head slightly, a small smile tugging at the corner of her lips. "That was just after you...got engaged, right?"

I blink, surprised. "Uh, yeah. How did you—?"

"Oh, I remember." She cuts me off, her gaze still fixed on the photo. "Jack's always loved Costa Rica. He talked about taking someone there for years. Never said who... but I guess I know now."

Her words hang in the air, laced with something I can't quite name—nostalgia? Resentment? I shift uncomfortably, unsure if she's being sentimental or if there's something more behind her knowing smile. How could she know about Jack's plans? He'd never mentioned discussing them with her.

She glances over at me, her eyes sharp, like she's reading my mind. "Some places hold a lot of memories, don't they? Some things you just...never forget."

I gaze over at Jack, and he's puffing out air, looking like a blowfish. What's on his mind?

We're both exhausted from our trip and just want to relax. That's what we do on a typical weekend—relax, since our weekdays are action packed.

Evelyn, on the other hand, is ready to party. Once she is properly oriented in the house—or at least on the first floor—she makes a beeline for the kitchen and approaches the wine cooler. She scans the variety of wine bottles and traces her index finger across them. "Hmmm, what's good here?"

Jack and I look at each other, and I involuntarily roll my eyes. Having wine while exhausted is not my idea of fun and relaxation. I fully expect Jack to intervene, but he just sits back on the couch and lifts his feet up on the coffee table.

Evelyn's having a full-on conversation with herself in the

kitchen, and we can barely hear her from the living room. But what I hear is her loud gasp proceeding, "Aha." She is excited about something. I come to the kitchen to inspect what she's up to. Apparently, she's pulled out the most expensive bottle from the cooler. In fact, it's one of the most expensive bottles in the world. A wedding gift from Jack's billionaire client.

Evelyn reads the label on the bottle, "Domaine de la Romanée-Conti Grand Cru 1945. Oooo, this looks delicious."

The wine name causes me to jump into panic.

I shoot Jack a look of disproval. He can see me, even at a far distance, but he says nothing. I'm peeved because he and I have decided we would have that wine bottle on a special occasion, and the day my mother-in-law arrives here, unannounced, is anything but.

Jack's client, who doesn't know what to do with all his money, bought it at a record-breaking $558,000 at auction in 2018. He knows that Jack and I go overboard when it comes to finding good wine. Despite our healthy wages, though, we could never afford something this expensive. This rare Burgundy is known for its exceptional quality and rarity, with only 600 bottles ever produced.

Evelyn puts the bottle on the kitchen counter and proceeds to look for a bottle opener, opening all our kitchen drawers. Jack stands up from the couch and leaves the room to store our luggage in the bedroom, leaving me alone to deal with her.

I spring forward to stop her, my heart in my mouth, but Evelyn has already found the bottle opener and, while humming through her nose, she begins to clear the wrap around the bottleneck.

I clear my throat. "Sorry, Evelyn." My voice is not overly harsh, just confident. "But that bottle...we can't open it now. Jack and I plan to have it on a special occasion."

Evelyn sharply turns around on the ball of her heels and gives me a solemn, wide-eyed stare. "Excuse me? Are you saying my visit isn't an occasion special enough?"

My shoulders slump, and I shake my head, trying not to roll my eyes. "Sorry, I didn't mean it that way. It's just that..."

The air is thick with tension.

"Well, what did you mean, then?"

"Forget it!" I wave my hand in dismissal, hoping she will let it drop and that this would be the end of it.

As I reach for the bottle, Evelyn lets go, but it barely grazes my palm before slipping away. It crashes to the floor, shattering into a thousand glittering shards, the sound echoing through the house.

I want to scream, but I'm too shocked to make a sound. A knot tightens in my stomach.

Evelyn and I stand in silence, studying the aftermath.

Wine pools across the floor, glass shards scattered everywhere. There's no salvaging any of it.

When I look at Evelyn, she tilts her head and smirks—no hint of remorse, just amusement and satisfaction. Her reaction fuels my anger, but I hold my tongue. The broken bottle feels like a sign.

A bad omen, foretelling even worse things to come from our uninvited guest.

CHAPTER 2

AS I CLEAN up the mess from the wine bottle with shaking hands, I'm still in disbelief over what has happened. I've been dying to taste the wine, which promised a once-in-a-lifetime experience. But Evelyn has ruined it.

She didn't even flinch. She's now picked another, much less expensive bottle from the cooler and poured herself a healthy amount without offering me any. With a quick movement, she picks up the framed photo on the counter-top. "You guys are all over the house." She chuckles. "So cute."

Her voice drips with sarcasm, and she sounds nothing like a loving mother-in-law.

She puts the frame back on the countertop, trots to the living room, plops down on the couch and turns the TV on like she owns the house. She cruises the channels until she finds something that catches her eye, then makes snarky comments about the show, laughing to herself.

Jack joins us downstairs, looking somewhat disheveled. He stands in the middle of the living room, looking around as if he's lost. I've only ever seen Jack this nervous a handful of times.

He makes a beeline for the kitchen and pulls another wineglass from the cabinet before filling it to the brim. Jack has had little to drink in years, not since the incident. He only indulges on special occasions. He once told me alcohol muddles his mind, and he's better off avoiding it whenever he can.

Knowing this, I'm stunned when he lifts the glass, brings it to his lips, and downs the entire thing in one gulp. His eyes grow hazy and wet, but the alcohol couldn't possibly have hit him this fast. Something else is going on behind that unfocused gaze. He's not ok.

He grabs the bottle again and refills his glass. Then, with drooping eyes, he glances at me and mutters, "You want one?"

"No, thanks."

I can't dwell on that now. I finish cleaning up the mess in the kitchen, as tired as I am, and go to bed early, without saying goodnight to Evelyn. Jack says he's exhausted, yet he stays downstairs to catch up with his mother.

While getting ready for bed, I hear their muffled voices

downstairs. It's hard to tell what they're talking about, but I'm dying to know.

Jack has told me little about his mother, and I've never asked, because I'm not that invested, to be honest. And the things he has told me about her are buried somewhere in the depth of mind. But now that she's here, curiosity is getting the better of me. It's her demeanor that rattles me.

She is not just disrupting my new life with Jack, but she is doing it with a smile on her face.

It's no surprise this is the first time we've ever met. Jack has hinted twice in the past that he's had a rocky relationship with his mother—that's what I do remember. Now that he's married, I wonder if their relationship will change for the better. Maybe she's hoping that having grandchildren will bring us closer together, and we won't feel estranged.

If Evelyn feels sad about missing our wedding over a week ago, she hasn't mentioned it yet. Nor has she told us why she is visiting us, unannounced. And how was she still so mobile, given her medical issues that were supposed to prevent her from traveling? Perhaps the actual reasons will surface during her visit.

I can't hear their distant conversation; only an occasional laughter coming out of Evelyn's mouth.

Half an hour later, I hear steps in the stairway, then a chorus of "Goodnight." Both go to their respective bedrooms.

We've put Evelyn in a corner guest room on the second

floor, while our bedroom is on the top floor. Our house is narrowly built, like a true brownstone building built in the mid-nineteenth century. The staircase looks unsettling, because it's steep and narrow, but thankfully there's a railing to aid the walk.

Jack has mentioned several times that when we have children, we will probably move to a suburb near Boston, like Brookline, which is affluent and ideal for raising families, with an excellent school system. We love our brownstone, and the location is fantastic, but it's not the best place for children to grow up in.

But I haven't been completely honest with Jack. I've never told him I don't want children—at least not with him. He believes we're on track to build a beautiful family, convinced that everything will unfold as it should.

Now that my mother-in-law is here, I've had a monkey wrench thrown into my routine. My thoughts are consumed by her sudden arrival.

When Jack walks into the bedroom, his walk is wobbly from the wine.

I'm quiet, and I know I'll be unable to sleep for a long while yet. Jack stands near the window while taking off his clothes and sharply exhales.

"Hey," I say.

He turns around and looks at me. "Hey, you. How come you're not sleeping?" He slurs his words, but I ignore it.

I prop myself up and sit on the edge of the bed to turn on the lamp on the nightstand. "I wish I could. I'm a little shaken by the bottle, number one. And number two—"

Jack cuts me off. "Oh, enough with the bottle. I won't hear the end, will I?" Jack exhales sharply, like he's under a lot of stress.

"Jack, I hadn't mentioned it once. I'm just trying to say that your mom helping herself to things is not cool."

He purses his lips. "Let's not worry about the bottle, Emily. It's the least of our worries now."

As a lawyer, Jack is pragmatic and likes to put things into perspective. God knows how many times he's tried to tell me not to worry about things I can't control. When I feel too anxious, he's my voice of reason. That's what makes this relationship work. But what does he mean about the bottle being the least of our worries? Is there something larger?

"Well, I was looking forward to tasting the wine. Besides, like I said, your mother had no place rummaging through our stuff and taking things without asking first. Don't you think?" I feel like I need to repeat myself to drive my point home.

Jack says nothing.

I press further. "Baby, did you know she was coming to visit?"

He looks at me and says, with much conviction in his voice, "Honest to God, I had no idea. I totally would have told you."

Jack looks afraid. He has told me he believes in the "happy wife, happy life" saying, so he would do anything to be honest and keep any doubts about his character at bay.

But both he and I know this hasn't always been the case.

"Isn't it weird that she just shows up unannounced?" I offer.

He nods and turns back to the window. "Totally weird. My guess is that she feels guilty for not coming to our wedding, so this is her way of showing that she cares about us."

I'm genuinely confused. "Care about us? Why now? Where has she been for the past year and a half?"

A year and a half. That's exactly how long it's been since I met Jack.

"I don't know." He shrugs. "Things change when your child gets married. She wants to be there for us and be a wonderful grandmother when we have kids."

I say nothing. I guess that's a good enough reason to come around.

Jack walks up to the bed and lies down. I follow suit and face him. "So, do you know how long she'll be staying?"

He scratches the back of his head while staring at the ceiling. "That's a good question. My guess is no longer than a few days."

I smile, relief washing over me. "I can manage a few

days. Maybe we can take her on a duck tour or go whale watching."

Jack stares at me as if contemplating my idea. He comes near and kisses my lips. "That sounds good, honey. She'd love that, I'm sure."

Before we say goodnight, we chat like we always do before I turn off the lights. Shortly after, Jack is snoring in his sleep while his back is turned to me. I'm way too exhausted to still be awake, but I can't fall asleep.

The sound of that bottle breaking into pieces still echoes in my mind.

CHAPTER 3

TODAY IS SUNDAY. Thank goodness, because I've woken up exhausted. Between getting a little sleep the night before and dealing with jet lag, I just want the day to go as uneventfully as possible. We have nothing planned.

I stretch in bed, hoping it's enough to get the blood flowing. I want to ask what Jack's plans for the day are, but he isn't in bed. The shower is running in the bathroom. I turn around and look at the alarm clock on the nightstand—it's only seven. I rub my eyes and sit up, staring at the bathroom door. Maybe I should join Jack in the shower, but as soon as the idea crosses my mind, the shower stops.

A minute later, Jack comes out of the bathroom, seemingly surprised to see me awake. "Hey, honey. You're up?"

I look around. "I think so, unless I'm dreaming."

He laughs and dries himself with the towel before dropping it on the floor. This is where I'm sure he will come back to bed for at least a cuddle, but instead, he walks to the dresser to retrieve a pair of new underwear and an undershirt. I'm hurt but say nothing. I suppose the honeymoon phase of our relationship might already be over. Or the eerie presence of his mother in the house could be another reason Jack seems distracted and uninterested in our usual playful activities.

Jack puts on his clothes and tells me he's going to make coffee and breakfast.

"Oh." I say, trying my best to hide my surprise. As far as I know, Jack can barely boil water. "That sounds good."

He walks through the door, and seconds later I hear him say, "Good morning."

My mother-in-law is up. She must be an early riser.

Staying in bed is pointless. I get up and put on my clothes and trudge downstairs. On my way, I notice the door to the guest room is wide open. It looks inviting. Out of curiosity, I approach the room, tiptoeing so they can't hear me. This is my house, and I can do whatever I want, but I admit it's creepy spying on a guest.

But she is not any kind of guest. She is my mother-in-law, and I want to know more about her.

I approach the door and peek my head around it, looking around for any strange signs. A single suitcase sits next to the dresser, and her shoes sit beside it. I don't see any clothing items resting on the chair in the corner or on the bed. Except for the luggage and shoes, there isn't any other sign a guest is staying at our home or in this room. In fact, the bed looks untouched, as if she didn't even sleep last night.

I'm happy she's not a slob, at least. I smile at the thought and proverbially slap myself for thinking harshly about her unexpected visit.

Maybe it won't be as bad as I imagined it.

Now that I've crossed that mental hurdle, I promise myself to remain cordial with her. It's only going to be for a few days. I can manage. There's no other way to get to know or to discover her motive for coming here unannounced.

Just as I tiptoe away, I hear something—Jack's voice. It's low, hushed, coming from downstairs. He's talking to someone. My heart skips a beat, and I freeze by the guest room door, listening.

"It has to be this way," Jack mutters, his voice barely audible. "Don't worry, she won't find out."

An icy chill runs through me. Is he talking about me?

Then I hear footsteps up the stairs, rushing toward me.

I turn around and see Jack standing at the top of the stairway. It shouldn't, but his presence startles me as if I've been caught. And I guess it's true—I have.

He cocks his head. "What are you doing?"

"Nothing. I wanted to see if your mom needed more

towels, but I remembered I brought a whole bunch in the other day." I smile as I stand still.

He sizes me up and down. "Well, that's nice of you." He walks by me and goes up the stairs to our bedroom.

"Is breakfast ready?" I ask.

"Almost. I just need to get something, and I'll be right down."

I walk down one more flight of stairs, and as soon as I land in the living room, my mother-in-law peeks her head from behind a kitchen cabinet, giving me a quick wave. She's humming, and as I approach the kitchen, I see her fully immersed in making coffee and preparing food that would have been Jack's job. She walks back and forth around the kitchen, opening the fridge and helping herself to whatever's inside before dropping items on the counter.

She takes a bowl out of the upper kitchen cabinet to beat eggs. She has clearly already familiarized herself with where everything sits. Her comfort level is unsettling, as I don't picture a guest acting this way. Not even my mother-in-law.

As I approach the kitchen island, the sight of the kitchen produces a panic attack: it's a complete mess, quite the opposite from how she'd left the guest room. Something revolting is burning on the stove, producing a grotesque smell. Bacon? I nearly gasp when I see a broken egg sitting on the floor and nearly a dozen different dishes, all dirty, randomly stacked up in the sink.

Is she taking over my kitchen now? And where's Jack—wasn't he supposed to make breakfast? It's clear he's let her take control, and I don't like it one bit.

I clear my throat to draw her attention. Evelyn quickly raises her head in my direction, then goes back to doing whatever she was doing. "Good morning!" She sounds chirpy and energized.

"Hey," I say as casually as possible, but I want to scream.

With my extreme anxiety, a messy kitchen is the last thing I can handle. After running a catering business for over a decade, I've never seen such chaos in a kitchen.

Before I do something out of line, Jack arrives, holding his phone in his hand. His forehead creases when he notices me just standing there, clenching and unclenching my fists.

"What's wrong?" he asks.

I close my eyes and inhale deeply, then look at Jack. "Nothing."

I walk over to the kitchen cabinet and take my prescribed anti-anxiety medication. I keep it hidden because I haven't told Jack I'm on it—he doesn't need to worry. When I take it, I'm fine. It's when I don't I feel like I'm going to explode in tough situations.

I swallow my pill dry, swing around and storm into the living room, taking my laptop from the small table in the corner. I usually refuse to do any work on Sundays, but today is an exception. I need something to distract myself from watching my mother-in-law detonate a bomb in my kitchen.

Besides, I should check on the progress for an upcoming wedding. We'd received the order a few months ago, and I need to go over the menu with the client one more time before finalizing it.

In my line of business—food catering—I've learned that customer service is of the utmost importance. I understand people can be demanding, but I always customize my work to meet their needs and add a little extra to make sure they're satisfied. They always return. I own the business, so I need to do whatever I can to sustain it. Word of mouth has been my best marketing scheme.

I do my best to concentrate on my email, but I am so unnerved by the woman in my kitchen. I peek in her direction occasionally, as she continues to make noises.

Jack is sitting at the kitchen island and reading something on his phone.

While waiting for the eggs to cook, Evelyn stands by the island and runs her fingers along the counter like she's done it before. "This house has such a familiar feel, don't you think, Jack?" she says, almost to herself. Jack looks at her sharply for a moment, then glances away.

His back is turned to me, so I can't tell his face expression. He remains silent.

Moments later, Evelyn yells out, "The food is ready!" She calls us to sit at the dining table.

She carries the plates back and forth, setting food on the table with practiced ease. Evelyn moves through the space with a confidence that suggests she's fully in control. None of it sits well with me. But I quiet my mind and take deep breaths, reminding myself that I've promised Jack I'd do my best to accept my mother-in-law into our lives.

CHAPTER 4

EVELYN HAS PULLED out our fancy plates from the kitchen cabinet. Of course, she didn't bother to ask if that was okay.

Jack and I purchased that set of Herend plates to impress his most important client, splurging a staggering five thousand dollars. We haven't touched the plates since, using them only for special occasions, like when we cooked for Jack's client to persuade him to hire Jack as his lawyer. That dinner ultimately advanced Jack's career and positioned him as the frontrunner for partnership at his law firm.

They are delicate, but Evelyn handles them with indifference. I'm annoyed, but I say nothing, afraid of seeming ungrateful for Evelyn making breakfast.

We sit at the table and look at the scrambled eggs and bacon. A bowl of cut up fruit sits in the middle of the table.

We've had the fruit since before we left for Hawaii, so it looks wilted and old. The eggs look unappetizing, and the bacon looks blackish and burnt. I gaze at Jack, who is staring at his plate. He bulges his eyes and purses his lips as if he is contemplating how to tackle his breakfast.

I can't help but giggle at his expression. Jack looks at me and smiles. "Isn't this wonderful? My mom comes here for the first time and decides to make us breakfast?"

I can't help but sense a hint of sarcasm in his voice.

"Oh, it's the least I can do," Evelyn smiles at Jack.

We fall into silence and all pretend we're about to eat as we move the food with our forks around the plate.

Evelyn places her fork on the table, crosses her hands with her elbows resting on the table, then looks at me. "So, tell me all about your wedding. I know I missed it...but I'll make up for lost time."

"It was wonderful," I say. "We rented a venue up on the north shore. The place is called Gloucester. We took our vows with beautiful ocean views."

I omitted telling her I'd spent the entire morning of our wedding retching in the bathroom. In fact, I haven't even told Jack that marrying him made me physically sick, like when you realize you've made a decision that can't be undone, and your body rebels against it. I'd smiled through the ceremony, but deep down, I knew something was off. That feeling has never fully gone away.

But it was too late to turn back.

"Oh," Evelyn squeals and places her hand on her chest. "Touching."

Jack remains silent and places eggs in his mouth. He's chewing at a sloth speed and doing his best not to spit it out. He hates scrambled eggs.

"I wish I were there. Maybe at some point you can show me your wedding photos. What do you say?" She winks at me and smiles.

"Well, we're still waiting for our photographer to send them to us, but, yeah, absolutely. As soon as we get them."

"Wonderful." Evelyn sits back and leans against her chair.

We sit in silence, each of us staring at our coffee mugs. I search for something to say, but nothing comes to mind. Besides Jack, there's little we have in common to talk about.

Finally, remembering why she hadn't made it to the wedding, I turn to Evelyn and ask, "How's your health these days?"

I'm embarrassed to say that I do not know what health conditions had caused her to end up in the hospital recently. Jack has alluded to something serious, but I hadn't probed further. Why hadn't I asked? Would he have thought I didn't care enough? Shame bites at me.

"My health?" Her face stiffens as she gazes at Jack, then back at me. "It's fine, but I don't want to talk about it." She waves her hand in my direction while keeping her stare at the table. "To be honest, I'm glad I'm still alive."

We resume eating in silence.

Suddenly, Evelyn perks up, turns to me, and asks, "May I see your wedding ring?"

"Oh, sure."

I extend my arm, and Evelyn grabs it, squeezing hard.

"Good grief." She yelps.

She examines my rings with a scrutinizing gaze before shoving my hand away in disgust. Then, turning to Jack, she offers a smile that never quite reaches her eyes. "You must love her, Jack."

Jack looks surprised. "Of course I love her." He gazes at me and smiles. "Emily is the love of my life."

Evelyn chuckles. "Of course she is. In fact, I haven't seen you this happy since...you know."

She picks up her mug and sips her coffee while looking at Jack, who is fidgeting in his seat. Jack slams his napkin on the table, pulls his chair out, and heads for the kitchen. "Anyone want more coffee?"

"I'll have more coffee," Evelyn says in a singsong voice.

Jack returns to the table to retrieve his mother's mug, giving me a vile look. I haven't seen that look before, presuming it has something to do with my question about health. Maybe it means I shouldn't be asking her too many questions, period. I should just stick with small talk until she leaves.

He pours coffee and returns with a mug in each hand. He sits down, biting his lip and rubbing his face. There's a worried look on his face. Evelyn's eyes dart between Jack and me, and she has a smirk on her face.

Maybe I should say something. Anything.

"So, Evelyn..."

"By the way, feel free to call me mom." Evelyn cuts me off. I look at Jack, and he gives me a quick smile then sips his coffee, averting his gaze from me. "I mean, if you want to. I would completely understand if you didn't want to." She chuckles nervously. "I mean, you have a mom of your own, right?"

"Yes," I respond. "My mom is still alive. She lives in upstate New York." It's funny how she knows nothing about me, and vice versa, but we're supposedly family now. We have a lot of catching up to do.

"Oh, wonderful. Then I guess I won't expect you to call me mom." She breaks into laughter that sounds odd.

"Listen," I divert the attention from the mom talk. "Jack and I are wondering if you'd like to do some touristy things around Boston. We can take you to the Museum of Fine Arts if you're into paintings and such. Or...we can take you on a less serious journey and do a duck tour?"

Evelyn's eyes are enormous, and her mouth agape as she

looks at me, frozen, while I speak. She snaps out of her trance and waves her arm. "Oh no. No need to go an extra mile for me. We can just stay here and relax and get to know each other. Right, Jack?"

She looks at him while her eyes are still wide.

"Right," Jack says.

"Besides, I don't want to impose too much," Evelyn adds. "I came here to give you a wedding gift. I just couldn't contain myself and had to come all the way here and give it to you in person."

"Oh." I chuckle. "That's awfully nice of you, Evelyn."

I look at Jack, who says nothing and continues to sip his coffee.

"But I won't give it to you just yet." Evelyn beams with a strange enthusiasm that makes me question her motives. What kind of gift could she be bringing that needed to be handed in person?

We finish breakfast, and I stay in the kitchen to clean up all the mess. Thankfully, my anxiety medication kicks in right away, so my brain isn't as scattered with disastrous thoughts as it might be without it. Evelyn doesn't offer to lift her finger to clean up. I guess her "cooking" was enough of the kind gesture.

She and Jack sit in the living room in deep silence. It strikes me as odd, since it's been a while since they saw each other. Isn't there a lot to catch up on? It just tells me how strained their relationship must be. And I find it strange that Jack never addresses her as a mom. Always Evelyn. That says something about how he feels about her and their relationship, surely.

Sometime in the afternoon, Evelyn announces she's going to her room to rest up. She says she takes midday naps, because they keep her young and invigorated. Jack and I encourage her to do so, because at this time of day, he and I always take a walk around the neighborhood and chat along the way. We've done it since we met, even in the winter. It's a good way to get exercise in and say things we usually don't in the home setting.

Several minutes after Evelyn went to her room, Jack and I head through the door. The day is humid, but it doesn't deter us from walking.

Jack seems rattled. His stride seems a lot more forceful than usual, and I try to catch up to him.

"Hey. Slow down," I call after him.

He half turns to me and takes a brief pause. "Oh, sorry."

He seems different since yesterday. Perhaps he's processing the fact that his mother showed up unannounced, which seems like a legitimate reaction. Or maybe he's adjusting to being a newly married man. I realize marriage isn't the same as dating or being engaged; it requires hard work and sacrifice. You have to switch gears and almost become a different person. I should probably ask him about it.

"Is something wrong?"

He shakes his head. "Well, I really don't like when you ask Evelyn so many questions."

I snap my head in surprise and say, "What are you talking about? Questions? What questions?"

"I don't like you asking her about her health. Didn't you see how uncomfortable she was?"

"Jack, oh my God! I asked, because I was concerned about her health. I genuinely wanted to know!" I nearly squeal.

How's asking about someone's well-being frowned upon?

"Listen, I don't think you should be asking her too many questions, okay? She just had a difficult heart surgery and almost died. So, put it to rest."

"A heart surgery? Oh my God, Jack. I had no idea."

We walk in silence, fast, while I ponder what Jack just told me. I'm confused about why this is taboo, but I don't want to rattle him even more. "I have to say, though, she looks great for someone who just had a heart surgery."

He doesn't miss a beat. "Yes, well, she has a brilliant doctor who took care of her. Plus, I guess she was determined to get better fast."

"Good for her," I add, since I have nothing else to say.

"But, yeah, if you don't mind, don't ask too many questions. Evelyn doesn't like it."

Jack's request surprises me, but it does tell me something more about my mother-in-law. Despite her abrasive personality, she must have a sensitive side.

I take his hand in mine and look at him, plastering a smile across my face. "Of course, babe. I certainly don't want to aggravate you or your mom."

I don't want his mother to stand in between us now that we're married.

I keep in mind that her stay won't be long. I can pretend I'm okay with this odd request. Besides, if I am being honest with myself, I'm not too keen on getting to know her. I'm sure she is a fine lady. If she keeps to herself, and I keep to myself, we will have a splendid relationship.

CHAPTER 5

THE REST of the day goes by uneventfully. Jack and I usually curl up on the couch and watch our favorite shows, but with Evelyn around, that's impossible. Evelyn is like that annoying shadow that lingers just out of sight, always interrupting our moments of peace. Instead of laughter and shared commentary, the atmosphere is heavy with her presence.

Whenever Jack tries to make a joke or suggest a show, Evelyn chimes in with her own opinions, often derailing our conversations. I grow increasingly frustrated, wishing for a moment of normalcy. As the day drags on, I can't shake the feeling that her watchful eyes are scrutinizing everything we say and do, suffocating the easiness we usually enjoy.

In the evening, Jack orders takeout, because neither he nor I could handle another Evelyn-made meal. On Sundays, we avoid cooking, as we expect a busy week ahead. Sundays are meant for relaxing.

Around ten, after we finish dinner, I excuse myself and head to bed. Tomorrow, I will return to work, where I'll be managing a significant client—the daughter of Gerald Smith, the CEO of New Balance, who lives in the Boston area. He's a self-made millionaire, capable of throwing a lavish wedding for his daughter, making this a client I can't afford to take lightly. How we handle him and his wife could make or break my business, so I need to be meticulous about every detail.

The wedding of their daughter is just a month away, and they will host over five hundred guests. My crew and I were excited when we heard from the client—the daughter's mother—who became teary as she described the kind of wedding they envisioned.

The plans haven't been completed, and my assistant and my right hand, Claire, has waited for me to return from my honeymoon until all the plans are confirmed.

I wake up at six, a little earlier than usual. Jack is still sleeping, his back turned to me. I take a quick shower, put makeup on and dress for work, tiptoeing around so not to wake up Jack. Just as I reach for the doorknob and head out, Jack's coarse voice stops me in my tracks. "Emily? You're leaving already?"

"Yeah. I have a lot of work to do and I'm feeling a little anxious."

"Got it," he says. "Hey, listen. I have dinner with a colleague tonight, so I won't be coming home right after work. He's working on a tough case and needs my advice."

As a corporate lawyer, Jack has seen it all: from bankruptcy to shoddy deals to IRS issues—you name it. But the main part of his job is to set up corporations for success and make sure they don't get into trouble. When they do, that's when Jack works long hours and meets with his partner to brainstorm ideas.

"That's fine." In the back of my mind, I picture spending my alone time with Evelyn, dread washing over me.

I hesitate, then assure him the plan is fine. Not that I have a choice. Besides, I don't want to be a needy wife.

As if Jack read my mind, he says, "Maybe you can take Evelyn out to dinner if you feel like it?"

I nod. "I might do that."

"Come here."

I stiffen for a moment, but I comply. As I approach the bed, he jerks my arm, pulling me in closer. I land awkwardly, pain shooting through my wrist. Now my head is resting beneath his, and I meet his wide, fearful eyes.

"And don't do anything stupid while I'm gone," he finally says.

My jaw tightens. "What? Stupid? Explain yourself, Jack."

"It's nothing, Emily. Just let it go." His tone is clipped, and for a moment, I think I see fear flash in his eyes before he turns away.

Then his ominous expression changes and he puts a smile on his face, acting like the old, composed Jack. He gives me a gentle kiss on my lips and hugs me, but I don't reciprocate. I'm a little shook by what just happened.

I straighten up and sit at the edge of the bed, uninterested in getting his affection. "Listen, Jack. You've got to stop this obsession with me fucking things up with your mother. I really don't appreciate it."

I've rarely used my stern voice with Jack, but it is necessary now.

He releases a heavy sigh and shakes his head. "I'm sorry. I don't know what's got into me. I must admit Evelyn's sudden arrival doesn't sit well. But...I can hardly kick her out and tell her to go home. A couple more days and she will be gone, I promise, and we'll return to our newly married life."

I look at him and feel sincerity in his speech. I lean forward and kiss him. "That's what I like to hear. So, I guess I'll see you later tonight?"

"That you will do!" Jack says playfully.

"All right. See you later. And don't do anything stupid!" I quip, but Jack doesn't respond.

Downstairs, my mother-in-law is already up, reading newspapers at the kitchen island. We don't get newspapers delivered, so I immediately question where she got them from.

"Good morning." I step into the kitchen and quickly grab my anxiety meds.

Evelyn's face is buried in the newspaper, and she doesn't respond or look at me. She might be deaf, but I don't think so. Whatever. I head through the door and embrace the sunny day. Since I didn't make coffee like I usually do in the morning, I head to my favorite coffee shop around the corner and get myself a big latte. There's nothing more satisfying than being awoken by the delicious taste of caffeine.

As I head to our parking lot around the corner, I forget all about my mother-in-law. All I can think of is what lies ahead at work. And I can't wait to embrace the day.

CHAPTER 6

MY FOOD CATERING company is in Watertown, a small town just outside of Boston.

Having come from a small family—only me and my little brother—from Upstate New York, I didn't grow up with a lavish lifestyle. My mom was a teacher, and my dad had a job related to IT security. They instilled in me the value of self-reliance and taught me to earn what I wanted through hard work. The catering business idea came naturally to me.

I've always been a foodie. At age five, my favorite pastime was mixing the ingredients for cookies my mom made on special occasions. My love for cooking developed over the years, sealing it as my ultimate destiny.

But never in a million years did I suspect I'd end up opening my business in Boston. It wasn't my first choice—

heck; it wasn't my choice at all—but I had no choice. As they say, you go where the wind takes you.

After I graduated, I settled in a small apartment in Waltham and worked my way up until I fulfilled my dream.

My catering company has done well. The facilities are out of this world. It's got a high-end commercial kitchen, a storage area, a packaging and staging area and in the building's corner is office space.

I pull into our parking lot and see Claire's car. She drives an old jagged-up Subaru, revealing her modesty.

Claire is easily one of the best employees I've ever had. She's smart and dedicated, and I can trust her with my life. Having been here since the beginning, she's well-versed in the art of catering. She makes me laugh at the most stressful of times. She is part of the reason I love what I do.

I go straight to my corner office and place my laptop on my desk. Minutes later, Claire comes in, holding her gift. She gives me a big hug and congratulates me once again.

I sense concern in her expression, but I don't ask. Not yet.

She dives in with questions. "How was the wedding?"

"Oh my God, it was the most magical experience ever. We had such a great time." I beam.

"I'm so sorry I missed it. I can't believe my babysitter canceled on me last minute."

Claire is a single mom of a two-year-old, and despite

juggling things in life all the time, she never misses a beat at work. I respect her for it that much more.

"I'm sorry, too. I know we said no kids at the reception, but I could have made an exception if I knew."

She waves her hand. "Oh, no worries. It's the thought that counts."

Claire fidgets in her spot and barely meets my eyes. What is she worried about? I can only assume it's related to her personal life. Maybe her kid is sick, and she needs to take time off. I really hope it's not a disaster.

"How was the honeymoon?"

"It was the best. If you haven't been to Hawaii, you should. It's heaven on Earth. Jack and I were talking about retiring there when we get old." I laugh.

My stomach twists. I can only pretend I will grow with Jack into retirement.

Claire only smiles and says, "Girl, you're already thinking about retirement?"

"Doesn't everyone dream about early retirement?" I quip.

Claire walks up to the chair. "Mind if I sit down?"

This is weird. I've never heard Claire ask if she could sit down. Our relationship is casual, more like a friendship, so I don't know where this is coming from. My assumption must be correct. There's something that bothers her and wants to get it off her chest.

She gets comfortable in the chair and looks at me. "So, I got a call this morning."

"A call?" What the hell. We get calls all the time. She's overly dramatic, and I suspect it's more serious than I'd initially thought. "What call, Claire?"

I lean forward and place my arms on my desk. Her tone and look make me nervous.

"A call from Gerald Smith. Actually, I tried to call his wife first to discuss some more details, but fifteen minutes later, he called."

My eyes widen in anticipation of Claire's next words. "And?"

"I don't understand why you canceled their wedding order, Emily." Her face darkens and her tone sounds scolding.

I gasp, and the air is knocked from my lungs. "What?" My voice sounds panicky. Squeaky. And I can't think straight.

This is our biggest client to date and a great opportunity to shine and elevate the company to the next level. It's a client like Gerald Smith who could help bring along an early retirement.

I shake my head in dismissal and finally muster, "Say that again?"

"Gerald Smith called this morning to ask why you sent him an email yesterday to cancel his order. He sounded really pissed, because he said it would be hard to find another caterer at short notice."

A lightning shock courses through me. I sent an email yesterday? How could it be? I don't remember such a thing, and besides, why would I do that? I would never, in a million years, jeopardize my reputation.

"I never emailed him, Claire. He's lying."

"Why would he be lying?" Claire has a point.

"I don't know. Maybe because he found a better deal somewhere else?"

"Seriously? He could afford to buy a small country. Money isn't his biggest concern." She points at my computer. "Well, you can always go to your sent box and check for yourself."

In the frenzy, I haven't even thought to do that. This is why Claire will always be an asset to my business. She's smart and logical.

"Great idea."

I open my laptop and type in my password, but the darn thing doesn't work because my hands are shaky. I breathe in and out and try again. Seconds later, my laptop comes at a full display, and I hurriedly open my email and head for the Sent folder.

My eyes dart all over until I spot the email to Gerald Smith. Right on top. The last email sent. Yesterday.

I hover over the email, feeling the heart thumping in my

chest. I am a few seconds from the evidence I might have just lost our biggest client ever. I read the message.

Dear Mr. Smith,
   We regret to inform you we must cancel the order
for your daughter's wedding.

"Oh my God," I say involuntarily. As I read further, my heart sinks deeper.

Matters come up unexpectedly and we are very sorry
to do this on a short notice. We will be happy to assist
you with any future needs. Good luck, and congratulations on your daughter's wedding!
   Sincerely,
   Emily Ross

"Fuck!" I stand up and walk away from my computer. "No, no, no!"

I sit back down and start checking my emails obsessively, hitting refresh over and over, scanning each one for signs of interference. Every delay, every unusual subject line, makes me wonder if someone was messing with me. I don't want to admit it to Claire or myself, but paranoia is creeping in. Am I losing it, or is something actually wrong?

A terrifying sense of doom washes over me as the reality sinks in. And then, like a little patch of blue sky in the stormy clouds, it occurs to me this is some kind of spoof only my mother-in-law could pull off while I was out on a walk yesterday.

"Claire, I didn't do it." I say, on the verge of tears.

Claire says nothing and stays put. We fall into deep silence until I calm down and can breathe again.

CHAPTER 7

"LISTEN, Claire, I didn't send this email, I swear." I'm totally shaken.

Claire just stares at me with a raised eyebrow. She looks petrified and curious at the same time. "Okay."

She looks like she wants to believe me, but I know that any explanation I could give her would seem far-fetched, implausible. The only way it would make sense is if I did it in some sort of confused trance. Jet lag and exhaustion can really take a toll on the body.

"I think it's my mother-in-law," I finally say.

"Your mother-in-law?" I don't think Claire meant to sound as shocked as she does.

"When we came back from our honeymoon, my mother-in-law was waiting for us at the door."

"What? Are you serious?" Claire's voice pitches high.

"Dead serious. What's more, this is the first time I've ever seen her in my life. I know nothing about her."

"So, you're saying she came to your house unannounced?"

"That's what I'm saying, yeah. I left my computer open in the living room. I wonder if she went into my email and sent it to Gerald."

"Wow." Claire's mouth falls open.

Exasperated, I turn to her and ask, "What should we do? Should we call Gerald back and tell him it was done in error? Maybe we can tell him it was an automated message that was sent to him by accident?"

Claire's eyes light up. "That's not a bad idea. How about we offer them a discount, too?"

I sigh in relief. Claire is a brilliant thinker and problem solver. "That sounds good. We can do a 20% discount."

It's a significant sacrifice, but I'll do anything to save my reputation.

"I'll call them," I tell Claire. I need to do my part as the business owner.

"Sounds good. And your mother-in-law?" Claire looks curious. "Tell me more."

I scoff, "She missed our wedding, and maybe she felt bad? I guess she's hoping we'll have kids soon, so she can take on the role of a grandmother."

Claire's brows stitch together. "Weird."

"She also said she had a wedding gift for us she personally wanted to deliver. But she still hasn't told us what it is."

"Hm. Yeah, that's weird, too," Claire repeats.

Her suspicion seeps into my psyche and makes me doubt everything about Evelyn's arrival even more.

I can't agree more with Claire, but I still challenge her. "What's so weird about that?"

"First, it's not like you guys will have kids tomorrow, right? I mean, you just got married and came back from your honeymoon. And second—the gift? That just sounds like some kind of excuse."

I pause and think about Claire's words. I guess she's right. Only a very selfish person could pull off something like that.

"Luckily, she's staying only a few days." I say, doing my best to abate her doubts.

"That's what they all say," Claire mumbles.

"Excuse me?"

"Nothing. I'm just teasing. I'm sure your visit with your mother-in-law will be fine," she says, putting on a fake smile. "Come here."

Claire walks up to me and pulls me into a hug, giving me a firm, quick squeeze. "Now, go call Gerald. There's not much time to waste."

When she leaves my office, all I can think about is the sent email. Could it really be Evelyn who did it?

I trace my steps from yesterday once again, and reason that Evelyn must have done it when Jack and I went for a walk. My computer is not password-protected, since Jack would never snoop around.

It had to be Evelyn.

Anger surges inside me as I realize how stupid and gullible I've been. Evelyn didn't come to repair her relationship with us.

She came to destroy us.

CHAPTER 8

DURING MY WORK HOURS, I sneak out to see my therapist, Dr. Whitman. She's just around the corner, a brisk walk from my office. My fear of Jack spotting me entering her building paralyzes me every visit, so I walk through a hidden alley between two buildings leading to her office, ignoring the stench of piss and garbage nearby. Jack doesn't know I've been seeing a therapist for over a year now.

But I have to keep seeing Dr. Whitman, I remind myself. It's the only way I can keep my impulses at bay and divert myself from inflicting danger. Though I've told Dr. Whitman several times already that I'm not planning on inflicting any physical harm on Jack. Much better to sabotage his career and make him suffer, sucking him dry in the end. It's the punishment he deserves.

Dr. Whitman is a kind woman in her fifties, with an

empathetic face. Her glasses, always perched on her nose, make her look scholarly and well read. Many times, she has busted out quotes from classics when she reflects on things. Her favorite quote is from Shakespeare: *It is neither good nor bad, but thinking makes it so.* Then she extends the thought by analyzing my thought process and offering sage advice.

Emily, you need to think about the consequences of your actions.

Dr. Whitman's office smells like candy, what I assume is the attempt to drown out the smells of fear and anger and the worst possible feelings that come out of her patients during the sessions. Her office, albeit small, is a sanctuary that has an easy way about it and forces me to say whatever's on my mind.

Today is no exception.

I plop on the couch across from her and sigh. Today proves to be entirely different—Dr. Whitman has deeper concern on her face, and she refrains from providing quotes.

"Well, hello, Emily. Good to see you."

"Good to see you, too, Dr. Whitman."

"You just returned from your honeymoon?"

"Yes," I say while fidgeting.

"So, how was it?"

"It was okay, given the circumstances."

"Just okay? Do you want to tell me more?"

"It's really hard to accept Jack and I are married now. If

you get my drift." I chuckle nervously. Dr. Whitman's face expression doesn't change, as she listens intently. "But I have no choice, you know. This is the only way to get close to him."

Dr. Whitman puts her hand down on her lap. "And this closeness? How does it make you feel?"

My eyes roll in my sockets and loop upward to one side as I consider her question. I shake my head, not fully knowing how to answer. But Dr. Whitman is patient. She has always allowed me time to think and process my world in real time.

"Well, I'm a little scared, to be honest. What if Jack changes suddenly and makes my life miserable? What if he discovers what I know about him and..." my thoughts drift away.

"Emily, last time you mentioned that marrying Jack was part of a plan. You felt it was necessary. Can you tell me more about that?"

I cross my arms, hesitating. I am not even sure how to best explain it. I sigh. "It sounds ridiculous now, but... marrying him seemed like the only way to get close enough to him. Close enough to finally make him feel what I've felt."

"What is it you wanted him to feel?"

I pause and think, studying my sweaty palms, "Power-less. Like everything could be ripped out from under him. The same way he did to me, once."

"You say he took something from you? But instead of distance, you chose marriage. Why was that, Emily?"

"Marrying him gave me access to his life, his vulnerabilities, his secrets. Jack is so confident, so in control of everything. I wanted him to know how it feels to be controlled, to have his life disrupted by the unexpected."

Dr. Whitman nods. "I see. And you thought marriage would do that?"

"Yes. He would never see it coming from his own wife. I could work from the inside."

Dr. Whitman leans forward. "That's a big commitment, Emily. To marry someone just to get back at them. Do you worry about how this might affect you?"

I shrug. "I knew it wouldn't be easy, but this was never about me being comfortable. Jack needed to feel the consequences. He needed to realize that I'm not someone he can just...discard or lie to."

Dr. Whitman pauses. Her forehead creases as if thinking hard. "And in pursuing this, are you sure you're not sacrificing a part of yourself?"

I swallow. "Maybe. But I can't let him walk away unscathed. It's too late for me to care about anything else."

Dr. Whitman's expression darkens. She leans in closer, her gaze locking onto mine, unblinking.

"Emily, I must say, this is some serious and heavy stuff." She looks at me, her brows slightly raised. "You're now married to Jack, and you've agreed to a lifetime of partnership. It's not a small feat to get married. The most understanding response would not be to marry someone under false pretenses, but take it to court...or whatever. Have you ever consider doing something like that?"

"No." I shake my head. "I really prefer to handle it myself. He's been cordial and doesn't suspect anything." I pause. "In fact, I really think he loves me."

Our feelings will never be mutual, but his adoration for me has made things easier.

"Emily, I think we still need to learn why you like to play with fire instead of just coming out clean."

I chuckle, "You don't understand, Dr. Whitman. He's a powerful figure. It wouldn't do anything."

Dr. Whitman stares at me and says nothing. Her concern for my state of mind is palpable. We've had similar discussions so many times, and nothing ever gets resolved. I'm the same stubborn Emily, and Dr. Whitman is the same concerned therapist. Her face looks even more worried and intense now that Jack and I are officially married.

I watch Dr. Whitman's every move, because she's the only moving object in the stifling room. She now places her hand on the chair armrest and fondles the top lightly with her fingers. Is she nervous?

"I'm concerned about this whole situation, Emily. I'm

afraid you will do something you will regret later. If you know what I mean."

I've always appreciated Dr. Whitman's sharp sense of observation, but sometimes she can be downright judgmental—worse than that prick of a show host, Dr. Phil.

I exhale sharply. "No, I won't go far. I just need him to learn his lesson."

Dr. Whitman moves her hands together and laces her fingers in front of her face. She exhales and looks at me scoldingly, like I'm her disobedient child.

"Emily, I want to be clear that I'm required to report any incidents that suggest an intent to harm yourself or others."

I smile. "Don't worry, Dr. Whitman, I won't do anything stupid. Besides, even if I wanted to, I can't. My mother-in-law is visiting."

"Your mother-in-law?" Dr. Whitman sounds surprised as she looks.

"Yeah. She arrived two days ago."

We sit in silence as she processes this new info. "Do you want to tell me more about her?"

I shrug. "There isn't much to tell. She seems...okay. A little too loud for my taste, but I think she'll be fine."

I don't tell her about the email incident, fearing Dr. Whitman will call me paranoid, among the other adjectives she has already called me.

Dr. Whitman nods slowly, her eyes moving around like little balls in a pinball machine.

I continue, "She tries hard, I guess. She made us breakfast yesterday morning." I don't tell her she made us scrambled eggs, a strange choice for Jack, who hates them.

"How well do you know her?"

I laugh. It must sound so odd to others that I hadn't met her before the wedding. "Not at all. I just met her."

"Okay. I'm assuming you will spend some quality time getting to know each other."

"Sure." I don't want to tell Dr. Whitman I have no interest in getting to know my mother-in-law better. I want her out of our house as soon as possible.

"And how does it make you feel that Jack's mother's here, but you're still having conflict with your own mother?"

I roll my eyes. My mom and I have had our fair share of disagreements, and I've always been the rebellious daughter she wishes she didn't have. She came to my wedding, but our relationship is far from warm and fuzzy. She doesn't like the choices I've made in life, and she keeps her distance to preserve her own health and sanity.

"It doesn't make me feel like anything. It is what it is. Besides, she's not staying long. Four days, tops."

"I see."

Dr. Whitman crosses her left leg on top of the right one and starts rocking it.

"Jack obviously has his mother to look after him. I think it's time you build your own support system. Obviously, you've seen me for a year now, but I think you need to move your focus onto something else and not ruminate over your marriage. Do you have any friends you can spend more time with? Relationships make life meaningful."

As soon as Dr. Whitman says it, I go over all the friends in my head like a slide show. Well, there's Jenna. And then there is Marcia, who moved to California years ago. But other than Jenna, I don't have many friends.

There's also Claire, but she's more of a coworker, a single mother with a two-year-old. Can I really expect her to step in to support me when she already has so much on her plate? She's overwhelmed with life as it is, and I don't want to burden her with my problems.

"That's a good point, Dr. Whitman. I should probably rely more on my friend...sss." I add the "s" in the end, so she doesn't think I'm a total loser.

"That's good to hear, Emily." Dr. Whitman uncrosses her leg and leans forward. "If you don't mind, I'd like to see you twice a week from now on. Is that okay?"

"Yes. Sure. I think I can clear my schedule for this week. When is good?"

Dr. Whitman stands up and grabs a notebook from her desk. She flips the pages until she lands on this week's calendar. "How about this Friday? Is Friday good?"

I check my phone, and it seems like my morning is wide open. "Friday sounds great."

"That's great, Emily. I'm glad you're agreeable to this plan."

Dr. Whitman's voice sounds grave and urgent. I bet if she could, she would see me every day, given what she knows.

CHAPTER 9

IF MIRACLES EVER HAPPENED, today would be the day. Gerald Smith agreed to stick with the contract, even though he sounded skeptical at first.

Disaster averted.

But I still have to confront Evelyn when I get home and give her a piece of my mind. I'm quite sure it's her who sent the email. And most importantly, I need to take charge of the situation before Evelyn destroys everything in her path.

Claire has to be right. Evelyn has a motive for coming unannounced. According to Jack, I'm not supposed to ask any questions, which makes this whole situation even more aggravating. I'm dreading the confrontation, but it must happen.

That evening, I stay at work a little longer, not just to

catch up on things but because Jack has texted me to inform me he will be home later than he'd thought.

I roll my eyes as more dread comes over me.

Jack doesn't ask how my day is going, or whether I'll be fine staying alone with Evelyn. I guess he only expects good things to come out of her visit; which, so far, has proven to be the opposite.

Claire leaves the office at six, in a hurry to pick up her son at daycare. Despite her responsibility as a single mother, Claire is available 24/7 and responds to my phone calls or texts right away. She says she likes to hear from me after work hours, because it makes her feel less lonely. Being a single mother does that.

When the darkness falls, I opt to go home with a churning stomach, knowing an unpleasant scene is about to be unleashed.

I drive through the city, but every inch closer to home makes me feel anxious. I grip the wheel tight and twist it like I am about to squeeze a lemon—as sour as I am.

Most of the windows of our townhouse are dark except for the ones in the living room. The lights are off, but it looks like the TV is on.

I burst through the door, instantly met by a wave of loud noise.

Evelyn has hooked her phone to our Bluetooth speaker

and has "Should I stay or Should I Go" by The Clash on a full blast.

She's standing in the middle of the living room and awkwardly swaying from side to side, attempting a dance. In her hand is a glass of wine, almost empty. The Persian rug is visibly stained, but it doesn't seem that Evelyn cares—she seems to be trapped in her own world.

Anger rushes through me.

"What the hell?" I mutter under my breath.

I drop the car keys on the little table in the hallway and run to the speaker to shut off the music. She comes out of her trance and finally spots me standing a few steps from her.

"Oh, hi."

She looks completely oblivious. Her lips are red from wine, and her hair, disheveled.

Evelyn approaches the couch and plops down, then stares at me and smiles. It's obvious she's tipsy. She says nothing.

I place my hands on my hip and stand in the living room, where Evelyn danced just minutes ago. The more she looks indifferent, the more my anger bubbles up inside. "Why did you send that email, Evelyn?"

My voice is loud and shaky from the effort of constraining myself not to do something stupid, like knocking that wineglass out of her hand or her teeth out of her mouth.

She looks at me with a wide-open mouth, but that expression of shock doesn't quite reach her eyes. She's faking it.

"What email?" She creases her eyebrows, seemingly annoyed about the question.

"The email you sent to my client!" I'm screaming at the top of my lungs.

Evelyn is mute.

She turns to watch the TV and lets out a loud laugh in response to a scene.

"Answer my question already!" My screams continue.

Evelyn turns to me with a smirk, clearly relishing in my weakness. I immediately regret my reaction—she has me right where she wants me. But I can't help it. Her cold indifference is driving me mad.

I trot to the light switch, flip it, and turn around to see Evelyn squinting at the brightness. But she maintains her eyes on the TV, still ignoring me. It's as if she knows how much I hate being ignored.

I locate the TV remote and turn off the TV. Evelyn flinches and fidgets in her seat, then looks me straight in the eye. But she still says nothing.

Since she's clearly reluctant to admit what she's done, I take it up a notch with my questioning.

"Why are you here, Evelyn?" My voice is forceful.

She shakes her head and rolls her eyes. "You have a problem with that?"

"Are you here to test me? Huh, is that it? Are you here to see if I'm going to break and do something out of line?"

Evelyn laughs.

"It's not funny! Because if you continue this behavior, I will!" I hadn't realized my voice could carry this far, but it does.

Moments later, the front door opens, and Jack appears in the living room. "What's going on here?"

Jack looks like he's been drinking again, slipping back into a bad habit he's fought to avoid for years. His words slur as he speaks, and the smell of alcohol clings to him. His eyes look hollow when he gazes at her, then at me.

Evelyn is still sitting with her legs crossed, then she crosses her arms, too, and scoffs, "Your wife here...is going nuts."

"What did you say?" I scream.

Jack approaches me, attempting to give me a hug to calm me down. "Hey, hey, hey..."

I yank his arms out of my way and point my index finger at Evelyn. "She..." I'm so angry I'm nearly lost for words, but I quickly gather my wits. "She emailed my biggest client, canceling the order, and now she pretends she didn't do it. The nerve of this woman!"

Jack tries to keep peace, but he seems out of sorts. "Baby..."

"Don't baby me, Jack. And look at our Persian rug. She's totally ruined it! She's ruining God damn everything!"

Evelyn turns to Jack, looking shocked, and says, as calmly as possible, "See what I mean?" She lifts her hand, examines her knuckles, tilts her head, and purses her lips. "I don't think I'm going to tolerate her behavior."

She presses her hands against the couch, pushing herself up to stand. As she walks past us, her voice remains eerily calm. "Good night. I hope you both sleep well."

Then she goes up the stairs to her room.

Jack turns to look at me. "Babe, what happened?"

I give him a mean stare. "Your mom..." I pause to catch a breath. "I'm pretty sure she emailed my client, canceling his order, pretending it came from me. I left my laptop over there."

We both look at the corner of the room.

"She must have snuck in and sent that email when you and I went for a walk yesterday."

"Oh, babe." Jack's shoulders slumped, his face etched in sympathy. "Let's go upstairs and relax."

By "relax," he always means something specific, but I'm not in the mood for it. Not tonight. And I hate that his mind goes straight to that rather than addressing my worries or confronting his mother over her behavior. He comes closer and lands a kiss on my lips. I purse my lips and feel the warmth of Jack's breath. I smell alcohol.

Jack grabs my hand, drags me across the floor, then up the stairs.

In the bedroom, we silently get ready for bed. But Evelyn's indifferent reaction is heavy on my mind. I won't be able to sleep until I talk things out with Jack.

CHAPTER 10

WE SETTLE IN BED, Jack turning toward me. I lie on my back and stare at a spot on the ceiling. The truth is, I don't want to look at him, partially out of embarrassment for my earlier reaction, and partially because, well, I don't want him to see I am still reeling about his mother.

She got me real good.

I vow to control my anger, knowing I come off as unhinged when I scream. The stakes are too high. I can't let this woman worm her way into my life and destroy everything I've built—not just my business, but possibly my marriage, too. I refuse to give her that power. I need to outsmart her before it's too late.

Jack puts the back of his hand on my cheek and comes closer. "What's the matter, baby? Do you want to talk?"

I turn toward him and give him a small smile. "Sorry, I

acted like a lunatic earlier. But your mom…"

I shake my head and turn back toward the ceiling.

Jack takes my hand and squeezes it lightly. "What about her?"

"There's no chance in hell she didn't send that email. But she's insistent she didn't do it, and it's driving me absolutely nuts. Why can't she just admit it?"

Jack pulls his hand away and retreats. "Are you sure you left your laptop in the living room? I don't remember seeing it there yesterday. Could your memory just be bad?"

I turn to him, widening my eyes. "What? What are you saying, Jack? Do you think I've made it all up? What the fuck!"

How much alcohol did he actually drink? It's clearly messing with his mind.

"Emily."

Jack tried to take my hand again, but I yanked it out of his way. Instead, I fluff the duvet in the air out of frustration. "You're taking your mom's side now? You think I'm crazy, don't you?"

"Emily!" Jack jumps out of bed and stands next to it. His arms are moving while talking, like he's Italian. "Don't you remember that time you left the front door wide open when we went to bed? You swore you locked it, but I found it wide open in the morning. We were lucky no one broke in."

I cross my arms in defeat and stare in front of me, pouting. I guess he has a point. My memory can be unreliable when I'm under too much stress or when I'm exhausted. Like yesterday after our honeymoon trip.

Jack sits on the edge of the bed and looks at me, forcing my eyes to meet his. "Emily, babe. I am not on her side, and I really want everyone to get along. Do you think we can do that?"

I shrug. "I guess."

"But I would never be on her side, silly. Besides, I want her to leave soon as much as you do, believe me." He chuckles. "Come here."

He approaches me and pushes me toward him to give me a hug. He caresses my hair in silence while we both sink, seemingly in deep thought.

Jack breaks our silence. "So, did Evelyn mention anything else?" My eyebrows stitch together in confusion. I free myself from Jack's hug and look at him. "Like what?"

Jack jerks his head. "Nothing, nothing. I'm just wondering if she said anything..." Jack clears his throat, "anything about why we stopped talking."

"No."

I tell him no, but now I'm doubting my memory. In that frenzy, we might have exchanged many more words I wasn't paying attention to, since I had a tunnel vision. If Evelyn had mentioned anything about Jack and her ceasing their communication, I've already forgotten about it.

"No," I repeat.

Jack takes my word for it, and his shoulders slump. His face relaxes. He lies back in bed and starts massaging my hand. He knows how much I love it when someone massages my hand. Jack does it so well that it's put me to sleep countless times.

"Is there something to be told?" I press on, my pulse quickening.

Jack stops massaging me for a split second. "No. I mean, yes, but it's complicated. It's nothing you need to be concerned about. Okay?" He comes closer and plants a long kiss on my lips. At least Jack is a great kisser, one silver lining in our marriage.

Minutes later, I'm in a better state of mind. I turn to Jack with a calmness in my voice. "A couple more days and she's going back home, right?"

He nods. "Yep. If everything goes as expected."

I want to ask him what he means by that, but I'm just too tired to carry on the conversation. I need my rest after a couple of tremulous days.

We finally say goodnight and turn our backs on each other. As I lie there in the quiet darkness, the weight of everything presses down on me, making sleep impossible. I am so consumed by this new reality that I completely forget to ask Jack how his dinner went.

CHAPTER 11

I'M GRIPPING the steering wheel, knuckles white, as the road stretches out before me. It's a long road I've seen many times but could never name. The sky is dark, and rain pounds against the windshield, making it nearly impossible to see. Suddenly, headlights appear out of nowhere, blinding me. My heart races, and I slam on the brakes, but the car skids out of control. Like in a bad horror movie, everything slows down—time seems to freeze as the car spins. I hear the crunch of metal, the deafening sound of impact, and the violent jolt of my body. The world flips upside down, glass shattering around me as I feel myself falling, weightless, until everything fades into silence.

I wake up, heart pounding, drenched in sweat.

Even after years, the recurring dream of car crashing still

rattles me. I take my time orienting myself, looking out the window. The sunshine outside makes everything seem better.

I do my best to push my bitter thoughts aside. The conversation I had with Jack last night finally sank in this morning as I lay in bed, meditating for a few minutes. I can tolerate a couple more days with Evelyn around. Nothing will come between us or weaken our marriage. Jack and I are solid, and Evelyn can kiss my ass if she tries.

While Jack is still sleeping, I sneak out of bed and do my usual routine in the bathroom. I tiptoe out of the room and trudge down the stairs. When I pass by Evelyn's room, I notice the door's cracked.

I stop by the door to listen in, and don't hear anything out of the ordinary except for water running in the shower. Evelyn's up already, even though she has no place to be or people to see. Why is she awake so early? I shrug my shoulders and continue down the stairs.

I walk into the kitchen, moving on autopilot straight to the cabinet where I stash my anxiety meds. The kitchen is the perfect hiding spot. My domain. In all the time we've been together, Jack has never cooked and doesn't even know where anything is.

He is the reason I take anxiety meds.

If he ever finds out, I'll just tell him that, one late evening a couple of years ago, I was almost robbed on the Boston Common, before we even met, and ever since have feared that someone is about to attack me, even in the daylight.

Anxiety meds have helped to abate the fear, and one pill every day does the job.

When I open the kitchen cabinet, I don't see it in its usual place. The hopeful feeling I had when I woke up is now replaced with dread. I stick my head inside the cabinet, searching for my pills, but they are not there.

I knock things over in my frenzy to find them, thinking I might have hidden them in a slightly different spot, but they are not in the cabinet at all.

This has to be another trick Evelyn has pulled off.

I erratically open all the kitchen cabinets before slamming them shut when I find no trace of them. My mind has hit panic mode. A sense of dread floods my mind, and I'm hanging on by a thread.

"Where are my pills?" I hear myself, but I don't know the meaning of the words or what exactly I'm saying.

My heart feels like it's about to burst out of my chest, and my head is spinning with fear.

It's one thing to be stripped of your lifeline—my medication—but quite another thing knowing that someone is playing the game. And it has to be Evelyn.

"Where is my medication?" My voice increases in

volume until I scream from the top of my lungs, "Where is my medication?"

My knees buckle, and I slide down the kitchen cabinet, landing hard on my rear. My face is streaked with tears, and my nose is running.

I cover my face as my body convulses with each sob, and I can't shake it off. Here is the living proof I need my medication. Stat.

Seconds later, I feel hands on my shoulders. "Sweetie, what is happening? What are you looking for?"

I remove the hands from my face and see the blurred Jack through my tears. I finally muster, "I need my meds."

Jack's brows crease, and he looks confused. "What meds?"

I realize I have more to explain, and I'm not sure how it will affect Jack's trust in me. We're supposed to share everything with each other—well, maybe not everything. But at least the big things that shape who we are. Now isn't the time to explain why I take anxiety meds.

"I need my anxiety meds. I can't find them anywhere!"

Jack kneels beside me, still confused. "Anxiety meds? You never told me you were taking those. Are you sure you didn't move them somewhere?"

His voice is soft but firm. I foresee a serious conversation soon.

I shake my head. "No, no, they're always in the same

spot. I keep them in the kitchen cabinet, behind the spices. They're gone. I swear, Jack, they're gone!"

"Okay, okay, we'll find them." He pats me on the shoulder like I'm a lost case. "You've been under a lot of stress lately, with Evelyn showing up and everything. Maybe you moved them without thinking."

"No! I didn't just move them. I'm telling you, Jack, they're gone. Someone took them! And it has to be her—who else would mess with me like this?"

Jack sighs and rolls his eyes, doing his best to calm me down. "Sweetie, you're jumping to conclusions. Let's not accuse anyone until we're sure, okay? Evelyn wouldn't do something like that."

"How can you be so sure? She's been acting strange since she got here. I don't trust her, Jack. She's trying to make me look crazy."

Jack rubs his temples. "Emily, listen. We'll find your pills, I promise. But please, don't start making accusations without proof. Evelyn's just trying to reconnect with us. She wouldn't—"

I cut him off. "You don't see it, do you? She's playing you, Jack. She's playing both of us. And you're falling for it!"

"Emily, stop. I know you're upset, but we need to stay rational. I'll help you find the meds, okay? We'll figure this out together."

My head whips around to face him. "Together? You're

not even on my side, Jack. You're defending her, and I'm the one losing my mind here!"

The voice behind us halts our conversation.

It's Evelyn.

"What's going on here?"

She is standing behind the kitchen island, staring down at us. Her arms sit crossed on her torso, and a towel is wrapped around her hair. She must have just gotten out of the shower.

Jack stands up and faces her. "Emily can't find her meds. Have you seen them, by any chance?"

"Me?" She points her finger at herself and rolls her eyes. "God, no."

She sounds nonchalant, but I can't help but notice a smirk on her mug.

"I came downstairs to see what the fuss is all about."

She turns on her heels and heads for the stairs. Does she really think I'm going to believe her?

I look down at my hands and notice them shaking. Jack stands up and starts opening the cabinets, looking for my meds. He opens the one above the coffeemaker. "Is this it?"

I turn to see him holding my meds high in the air. It's definitely them. I nod, immense relief flooding through me. I wipe the tears from my face and stand up to take the pills. Our eyes meet, and I see concern in his. I avert my gaze, swallow the meds, and thank him for finding them.

"I didn't know you were taking these," Jack says, with a creased forehead.

I tell him about the Boston Common incident, but he squeezes my hand in sympathy. I hope he doesn't suspect I'm bluffing. But how would he feel if he knew the actual truth?

CHAPTER 12

DESPITE HAVING TAKEN MY MEDS, I'm still reeling from the earlier experience.

I drive to work, but I barely pay attention to the surrounding traffic. The driver behind me honks when the traffic light turns green, but I remain idle.

Evelyn is heavy on my mind.

It's been only a couple of days since she arrived, but it feels like an eternity. As much as I'd like to give her my respect as my mother-in-law, I'm starting to feel an intense dislike toward her, and it scares the hell out of me.

My attitude needs to change, I get it, but I'm afraid that seed of doubt has already sprung up inside me.

When I arrive at the office, I text my best friend, Jenna. Dr. Whitman's words have stuck in my mind: *you need a support system. Hang out with your friends.*

Jenna and I have known each other since grad school. We both went to Boston University School of Hospitality Administration and have been besties since. We stuck around in Boston after we graduated, but Jenna had less luck in launching her own business. Instead, she works as a private consultant, advising local restaurants on how to run their business, put the menu together—all the works.

I am desperate to talk to her today.

She's one of those people who will ask as many questions as needed to understand a problem. She's quite opinionated. That trait has been annoying, but today, I wouldn't mind being interrogated. Maybe I will see things from another perspective, a more positive one. Because, right now, everything looks bleak as far as our guest is concerned.

I shoot her a text message:

> Hey, Jenna. Are you free tonight? I'd love
> to grab dinner and see you.

Nobody likes to be invited to a social gathering at a last minute, but Jenna and I have that kind of relationship. Besides, she's single and likes to be called out on a whim.

She texts back immediately.

> Yes. Name the place and time.

I text her back and tell her to meet me at Joe's, a popular bar a few blocks from my house. Jenna doesn't live that far from me, yet we rarely see each other anymore. She's just always so busy on weekends, it's impossible to plan anything.

I settle at my desk and check my email. Claire walks into my office, holding a cup of coffee. She drinks copious amounts throughout the day to stay perky and fresh.

After we've exchanged niceties, she reminds me we have a meeting with another big client tomorrow. If it goes well, it will position us to elevate our company and score some bigger events in the future. Claire is all excited, as she claps her hands, telling me all about it.

Before she heads out the door, I stop her. "Hey, Claire?"

She turns around, startled. "Yes?"

"How do you take showers when you're home with your kid alone?"

She snaps her head back, surprised at my question. "Ummm. I don't know. Most times when he naps."

"I see." I nod my head slowly.

"But my showers are usually rushed. I used to take long baths, but I don't remember the last time I took one."

"Oh," I say. "And what about if you want to go out for a beer with a friend? How do you arrange that?" I'm fast-forwarding to dinner with Jenna tonight and trying to picture how it would happen if I had kids. What would I do? Both Jack and I have busy jobs. Late nights are inevitable for us. It's a hypothetical, though. Jack and I won't have kids together.

Claire laughs. "Beer? What's that? I mean, nowadays, I don't socialize at all, but when I do, my next-door neighbor watches Scotty."

"Oh, okay." My mind churns.

"Why do you ask?"

"Nothing." I don't want to tell her the truth. It's hard for me to even acknowledge how much Evelyn's visit has been on my mind. I'm still trying to fit her puzzle piece into our lives to make sense of the bigger picture. Maybe it's true, as she says: she wants to be present when she becomes a grandmother.

"Are you thinking of having kids already?" She winks at me.

"Maybe." I smile.

"That would be great." She claps her hands in amusement.

I smile at her, but inside I feel conflicted. "Yeah, it will be."

"Oh." Claire seems to remember something important to say. "I forgot to tell you that our meeting tomorrow got moved to eight in the morning. There are a couple of people in Europe, so with the different time zone and all, they can't do it at the time we've scheduled."

"That's not a problem." I wave my hand at her. "I'll be here."

Claire and I are early risers, and we arrive in the office

first. She knows I live for this place. I'm not sure what her excuse is, especially since she has a small child.

"Get some rest, and I'll see you tomorrow."

I look at my watch and notice it's almost time to leave.

When Claire walks out of my office, I reflect on what she told me about her son. It's good to get a perspective on parenthood and family from her viewpoint.

But I'm looking forward to hearing it from my best friend, Jenna. She will tell me like it is.

CHAPTER 13

I AM RUNNING a few minutes late for my dinner with Jenna, so when I arrive at Joe's, she's already sitting at our table. She sees me at the door and waves at me, as if I haven't already spotted her. It's hard to miss Jenna anywhere.

She looks dashing. There have been many times I felt like an ogre next to Jenna. I am not bad looking by any means, but she looks amazing. She's wearing a black dress, revealing her cleavage; her makeup is immaculate, and her blonde hair looks like silk. A couple of jocks at the bar are gazing at her, because it would be hard not to.

As I approach the table, Jenna stands up and gives me a long hug.

"Hi, babe."

"Hey, Mrs. Ross." She smiles.

It's weird, but it's the first time I've heard someone call

me Mrs. Ross. The sound of it gives me this yucky feeling, like someone has tainted me with a label I didn't ask for. It's as if the name carries weight, expectations, and a history that doesn't belong to me, yet here I am, stuck with it.

We sit across from each other and smile awkwardly.

Jenna's gaze is filled with anticipation. She's probably eager to hear about what's so important that I requested to meet her at such short notice.

"How does it feel to be called Mrs.?" Jenna bites down on her lip and squints only so slightly as she waits for my answer.

Ever since I've met Jenna in grad school, all she's talked about is men. She's one of those women who can't stand being alone. It's like something is eating at her insides if she has to spend weekends alone.

Her biggest problem is choosing men who are not invested in their relationship as much as she is. When you don't have a good equilibrium in the relationship, it will tip over and finally break. I've told something like this to Jenna many times, but she just brushed me off. It's more important for her to not be alone than to spend on herself until she's ready to build a meaningful relationship with someone worthy of her time.

What's worse, Jenna and her meathead boyfriend, Gary, recently broke up, and she has been devastated. This last experience has rattled her self-esteem, and she's doing her best to pick herself up, brush herself off, and move on.

I consider her question, but I don't know how to answer it. It all sounds hollow, but I will pretend to be a happy bride. Or at least indifferent.

I shrug as I dart my eyes to the menu in front of me. "I don't know. About the same." I let out a nervous chuckle.

"Really? It doesn't feel different now that you guys are married?"

I shake my head. "I don't know. It's been less than two weeks. I mean, I'm loving it so far..." I pause and, while I contemplate my response, one thing creeps into my mind.

Evelyn.

She's like an annoying mosquito—hard to get rid of.

I shake my head to dislodge her out of it and continue. "It's great. And it's just the beginning. How are you?"

"Busy." She nods quickly. "I've been keeping busy. A bit of a wreck, you know." I know she is referring to the heartbreak Gary has caused. She swirls her hair around her index finger, then purses her lips and gazes down at the table before she looks at me again. "I'm just tired. I could use a vacation just about now."

"Oh." I touch her hand lightly. "I'm so sorry. Maybe you and I can do a girl trip down to the Cape, if you're up for it?"

But Jenna says nothing. She just laughs. In Jenna's

world, a girls' trip can never compete with spending time with a man.

The waiter interrupts our conversation, and we order drinks and food. I'm not feeling hungry, but I should munch on something before I down my martini. Or should I say, *martinis?*

Jenna resumes her thoughts. "I'm ready to date again, Emily. I'm a little tired of being alone."

Her eyes get bigger, and I can see the fear in them. I want to shake the shit out of her and tell her to slow down, but it will all fall on deaf ears, like many times before.

"Maybe I can ask Jack if he has a friend we can set you up with. What do you think?"

The moment I ask, I regret it. Jack doesn't really have any single friends—or many friends at all, for that matter. It's hard to maintain a social circle when you didn't grow up here. He moved to Boston for school and stayed after, just like I did.

He never wanted to go back to Seattle ever again.

"Maybe." She smiles.

I leave her with that thought and hurry to the bathroom. As I cross the floor, I can't shake the feeling that someone is watching me from outside. It's an unsettling sensation, like an instinctive awareness that danger is lurking, though I can't pinpoint what it could be.

When I return to the table, Jenna is talking to one of the

jocks at the bar, laughing, and handing him a business card. The mood lightens, probably because Jenna feels like she's scored. There are dating prospects in her near future again.

"You see—when you least expect it," I say.

Another hearty laugh comes out of Jenna. "So, tell me, what's going on with you?'

Finally.

I sigh and shake my head. "Oh."

I'm lost for words. Where do I even begin?

Jenna creases her forehead and leans forward. "What's wrong? Something happened between you and Jack?"

As she poses the question, I hear amusement in her voice, like she's happy that the drama is brewing at home. Concern is spread across her face, but it never quite reaches her eyes. She looks insincere. Or am I just imagining it?

Even the best of friends can sometimes secretly hope you fail, so you can join them in their misery. I'm not saying that's what Jenna wants, but I can't help but wonder.

But if I'm remotely close to the truth about how she feels, it's not what she thinks. I tell her all about my mother-in-law, hoping to glean her perspective on the situation.

"What? Are you serious? She just showed up at your steps like that?" Jenna's mouth is hanging wide open while she stares at me with her big brown eyes.

"Yep. But you don't know half of it."

I tell her about the broken wine bottle, the mysterious

email sent to my client, my misplaced meds, and our verbal sparring match from yesterday. She jolts against the seat and gasps hard. "Are you kidding me right now?"

I shake my head, "Nope."

"Wow, what a witch." Jenna grabs her wineglass and takes a healthy sip.

I scoff. "You don't have to tell me that."

"So, what are you going to do about her?"

The barrage of questions has begun. But I don't have the answers. This is where Jenna comes in. This is why we are here tonight.

"That's the thing. I'm at a loss. I'm trying my best to be cordial with her, but I have a feeling she's got another motive for being here. And I have no idea what it is. She says she can't wait to be a grandmother, but Jack and I haven't talked about having kids just yet."

Thank goodness.

"What does Jack think?"

"He believes she's here for good reasons. To patch up their relationship or something, so she can be the best grandmother she can." I mimic quotation marks for that last part and roll my eyes. The amount of alcohol is making me feel all sort of things, but none of them are comfort. "I guess they haven't been on good terms for a while."

"Why?" Jenna presses on.

I pause and think. "I don't really know. I just know that Jack is all about her being here."

"How long is she staying?"

"Well, she says a couple of more days. I guess I could tolerate two more days. But, you see, I don't want her to leave on bad terms. I don't know what I can do to make friends with her."

"I know what you mean." Jenna seems too excited about this recent development in my life. She's been all ears, and now I'm pretty sure she's about to land some advice on me. "Doesn't sound like you have a lot of time on your hands."

"Right."

"Well, here's what I would do if I were you."

"Do tell." I lean forward and eagerly anticipate Jenna's advice.

I'm desperate to do whatever she tells me.

CHAPTER 14

I COME HOME INVIGORATED and I skip and giggle like a little kid in a candy store. It's most likely the martinis talking, or it could be the fact that I have a plan now. It's all coming together, thanks to Jenna.

Jenna is a fresh breath of air, always full of ideas and energy. I vow to follow her advice this time, because I'm all out of ideas of my own. Sure, Jenna can be consumed with her singlehood and is so ditzy, so some might wonder if she's the best person to listen to. But back in grad school, Jenna always struck me as an intelligent woman, getting As and Bs all the time. Really, by listening to her, I've got nothing to lose.

I walk through the front door, excited to turn the new page, only to be welcomed by eerie silence, a stark difference from last night. Evelyn has been so unpredictable, so who knows what I'll get from her today?

"Hello!" I call from the hallway, but no one comes out from the corner to greet me back. Neither Jack nor Evelyn appears to be home. A pungent smell hangs in the air, leading me to believe that Evelyn must have cooked in the kitchen today. It smells like asparagus and pork chops.

I walk into the living room and drop my purse on the couch. I head to the kitchen to grab a glass of water to counteract my tipsiness when I encounter a horrible scene. If it previously looked as if Evelyn detonated a bomb in the kitchen, this time around, it looks like as if a nuclear war demolished the place. Not only are the floors dirty from food scrapes, spilled milk, and other unidentified items still lying around, but the sink contains a tower of dirty dishes that are about to tip over and crash.

But that's okay, I tell myself. Jenna's words recycle in my head like a broken record: *Be a better person. Take the high road. Give her the benefit of the doubt.*

Evelyn is leaving in two days, and God knows when I'll see her again. I'm spinning everything into a more positive note, like Jenna and I discussed.

Like Dr. Whitman wants me to be.

An open wine bottle sits on the kitchen island, and I consider having a glass, but the martinis have gotten to my head. I'd better not. I don't see any wine-stained glasses floating around, so I'm assuming Evelyn is somewhere inside the house with her glass.

She could very well be hiding in her room after leaving the kitchen in such massive disarray.

I go to the living room and lie down on the couch. It's nine in the evening, still too early to head to bed. As I place my head on the armrest of the couch, footsteps echo down the stairs.

It's Evelyn. She is holding a wineglass in her hand, her pinky sticking out.

I sit up to greet her. "Hi." I plaster a genuine smile across my face.

Be the better person. Take the high road. Give her the benefit of the doubt.

"Why, hello! You're home late tonight. Did the work keep you busy?"

Her tone is nondescript. I can't tell if she's genuinely interested in knowing, or if she's just trying to make a conversation.

"Oh, no," I say. "I had dinner with a friend from college. I haven't seen her since the wedding."

"I see." Evelyn walks to the kitchen to refill her glass, then yells out, "Who's your friend?"

Her tone remains calm and cordial. It feels like a ploy to divert from all the shit that's happened so far. But again, if I follow Jenna's advice, maybe all of it will somehow disappear into thin air and become a happy ending.

"Jenna," I say. "She recently broke up with her boyfriend, so she wanted to talk."

Evelyn sits in a recliner across from the couch and crosses her left leg over the other.

"Is that so?" She winks at me, as if I might have lied about Jenna. I tell myself arguing is pointless. I will just ignore her insinuation.

I nod. "Yes. She's my bestie from grad school."

Evelyn offers me a strange smile as she sips her wine, maintaining eye contact above the rim of her glass.

I wonder if Evelyn is in a relationship, or what her love life is like, but maybe there's an opportunity to find out soon.

"Hey, Evelyn. I was thinking that maybe Jack, you, and I can have dinner tomorrow night. There's a cute little restaurant in the North End I think you'll love."

Evelyn uncrosses her leg and leans forward. "I would love that."

She sips her wine, then smiles at me.

This will be a great opportunity to get to know Evelyn and her past with Jack. I'd love to learn more about how he grew up and what kind of mother Evelyn thinks she was. Maybe I'll also find out what has caused a strain in their relationship.

This is all Jenna's idea. Keep your friends close, enemies closer and all that.

"Excellent." I clap my hands in excitement. "I'll make a reservation for 7:30 tomorrow evening."

The front door opens, and Jack walks in.

He seems surprised to see Evelyn and me sitting in the same room and not arguing. I'd have thought that would make him happy, but he looks uncomfortable. After several awkward seconds of him gazing at me, then at Evelyn, he says, "Good evening, ladies."

"Hi, son," Evelyn says, her voice sweet. "How was your day?"

"Busy." Jack is short. He has clearly seen better days. It's as if stress has creeped under his skin and he's trying his best to shed it off. I imagine having his mother here, unexpectedly, has done a number on him, and he's straining to always be cordial and friendly.

He sits next to me, and as he usually does, he squeezes my leg for a quick second. His way of saying hello.

I turn to him. "Free all your plans tomorrow evening, because we're going to dinner at your favorite restaurant."

Jack gazes at Evelyn. "Okay."

Evelyn flashes him a quick smile, clearly pleased with the shift in tone. It's a welcome change from the accusatory, paranoid screaming that's dominated interactions since she arrived.

Besides, I'm in a good mood and have good news to share.

I was going to wait to tell them the news about my new client at the dinner tomorrow night, but I cannot contain my excitement. Plus, those two martinis got me all warm and fuzzy.

"So, I have big news to share."

Jack snaps his head toward me. "Yeah? What is it?"

"I'm signing up with another big client tomorrow. We have a meeting at eight in the morning to go over details."

Evelyn's eyes are enormous, and her mouth wide as she listens to me. Her face relaxes an instant later, and she says, "Congratulations, dear. We'll have to celebrate tomorrow."

Jack leans in and kisses me on the lips. "Way to go, babe."

"Thank you. I should probably go to bed early. I need to be in the office early for my call."

We say our goodnights and go to our respective rooms. Jack is quiet when we arrive in the bedroom. He doesn't ask the usual questions about how my day was, or how dinner with Jenna went.

Something must be bothering him.

Just before we turn the lights off and fall asleep, I put my hand on his cheek and look him in the eye, "Babe, something wrong?"

He gazes down. "No. Nothing wrong. Actually...I'm just

curious. Whose idea was it for us to go to the restaurant tomorrow?"

"Mine." My words come out more as a question than an answer. Was it a wrong thing to do?

Jack squints. "Why would you do that without asking me first?"

I remove my hand from his cheek, as if burned. "I thought you'd be more than happy I suggested it. Your mom is leaving soon, plus it would be nice to patch things up before she leaves. It's not like we started off on good terms. Don't you think?"

"Sure. But how would you feel if I organized dinner without asking about your schedule first? I bet you wouldn't like it."

Jack seems agitated, and I do my best to defuse the tension. Last thing I want is for Jack to turn completely against me. I need to tread carefully.

"Is this what it's all about?" I sigh and touch his hand lightly. "I'm sorry. If you can't make it, I can just cancel the dinner. Okay, babe?"

I lean in and kiss him on the lips. He kisses me back and gives me a quick smile.

"It's fine. I'll do my best to be there."

I nod. "Keep me posted."

Sleep doesn't come easily. I toss and turn, throwing around the idea that alcohol might be to blame. Past midnight, when I'm certain sleep isn't coming soon, and the house is eerily quiet, I head downstairs to clean the kitchen. Now that the alcohol has worn off, I stand in front of the pile of dirty dishes, reminded once again of what kind of mess I'm left to deal with—both in the kitchen and in my life. The stillness of the night amplifies everything, making it impossible to ignore the chaos brewing beneath the surface.

CHAPTER 15

THE HANGOVER MAKES my head throb when I wake up.

The sun's brightness feels offensive and doesn't help my headache. I reach for my anxiety meds in the nightstand drawer. After that dreadful experience yesterday, I wouldn't dare leave it out in the open again. I pop Ibuprofen, hoping the headache will be gone soon.

Today is the important meeting with my big client, so I need to be in the right headspace for it.

Jack is still sleeping. He's on his back, his face scrunched up as if he is having unpleasant dreams. I've occasionally heard him talk in his sleep, blurting out something about guilt and regret, but I don't pay much attention to it, nor do I ask. I leave him be.

Downstairs, I make a quick cup of coffee and get it ready to go, since I want to be in the office early and review the client information one more time. Everything needs to be perfect when we speak. There's nothing more annoying for the client than to be asked questions repeatedly. I always make sure to be a step or two ahead to impress my clients. Sometimes, it's as though I can read their minds, and they seem to appreciate it.

As I walk toward the parking lot, just around the corner from our house, a sinister feeling creeps over me. I can't explain it. I glance up at the sky, where a few white clouds rush past, and the humid air signals impending rain. Everything feels off, like I'm walking in shoes five sizes too big, constantly tripping over myself.

A minute later, it becomes clear.

The front tire on my car is unmistakably flat, a dizzying scene that immediately catches my eye. The car leans awkwardly to one side, where the deflated tire sits, pressing heavily into the asphalt. My heart sinks as I take it in, a wave of dread washing over me. The stark contrast between the flat tire and the rest of the car feels like an omen, and my mind races with the possible consequences. What if I'm stranded here?

And what if I miss my meeting with the client? I can't let that happen, but as I stare at the car in its useless state, panic sets in. My heart races, and my mind spirals, the worst possible thoughts burning in my head, clinging to me like flies to shit.

How long will it take to fix it? Worse, what if this wasn't an accident? The eerie feeling from earlier intensifies, leaving me paralyzed for a moment, the humid air pressing down on me, thick with unease.

How the hell did my tire get flat in the first place? Did someone purposely slash it? Boston has some dangerous parts, but Back Bay is not it.

The parking lot is gated and locked all the time, relatively safe and tucked in. Unless someone specifically targeted my car, I don't see how this could happen.

Or maybe I do, but I don't want to consider it.

I slouch to examine the damage, studying the tire more carefully. There's no doubt this was a deliberate attempt to sabotage me. The jagged tear in the rubber, too precise to be accidental, sends a chill down my spine. Someone wanted to stop me from going to my meeting with the client. Someone who knew about it.

There are only a handful of people who knew.

This realization gets me all rattled. I instantly look at my watch and, while it's still early, I'm still afraid I am going to miss the call. What the hell do I do now?

I can't think straight. I walk around my car to check out the other tires. Not that it matters, but they are all intact. Well, it takes only one to render the car completely useless.

Why? Why? Why?

"Ugh," I grunt. I'm still dizzy from the panic attack, and walk up to the street, feeling helpless.

Think fast.

There's no point in calling Jack to drive me to work. We own one car, since he takes public transportation to his office in downtown Boston, on Milk Street, a mere few miles from our house. My mind races between trying to figure out who could've done this and the pressing need to act quickly and find a way to get to the office on time.

I take a few deep breaths and massage my temples with my fingers, feeling the heat rushing to my head.

After opening the Uber app on my phone with shaky hands, I put in the address of my workplace, but, Jesus, there are no cars available in the vicinity. Where the fuck am I? Siberia?

"Oh, my God. What do I do?" I whimper, shake my head while suppressing the need to scream out of frustration.

It's only seven. I still have time. Or so I think.

I try Uber again, and relief is all I feel when my request gets accepted. There should be a car arriving in eight minutes. Eight minutes feels like an eternity, but it's better than being stuck here in the parking lot.

As I exhale a big breath, a renewed sense of vigor gives me hope. Until the worst happens—my Uber ride gets canceled. A notification in the app says that my stored credit card has expired, and I need to update it.

"Are you shitting me?"

Well, this is what I get for Jack, always insisting that he call for an Uber when we're out and about. I haven't used my account for a while, so it's no surprise that my information is outdated.

"Shit."

I slouch and place my purse on the ground, combing through my stuff, looking for my wallet. It's right at my fingertips, but I'm so rattled that I don't even notice it at first.

"Focus, focus."

I grab my wallet and pull a bunch of stuff out of it. My ID and all my credit and business cards are spread all over the ground.

I scramble to pick everything up, my fingers trembling as I shove the cards back into my wallet.

"Breathe," I mutter to myself, though the pounding in my chest is relentless.

My mind flashes to the meeting—sounds of the client's impatient voice, the disappointed sighs, losing the deal. The weight of failure bears down on me as I fumble to update the Uber app with my new card details.

Finally, the update goes through. I exhale sharply and check the app again—my ride request gets accepted. Five more minutes until the car arrives.

I stand there, clutching my purse tightly, staring at my car as it sits there, useless. Who would do this? Why today, of all days? I look around the parking lot, searching for any sign of who might be responsible. No one's around. The place is eerily quiet.

I look at the periphery of the buildings nearby to scan for security cameras, but I see none. I guess discovering the perpetrator is out of reach.

Maybe I should call Jack to talk things through. But what good would that do? He's probably getting ready for work, perhaps taking his long morning shower. And besides, what could he do to fix this?

As I stand there, my phone buzzes with a message from Claire:

> Everything set for your meeting at 8. Let me know if you need anything else.

It's seven thirty now. Will I even make it?

I swallow hard. Do I tell her I might not make it? The Uber's still four minutes away, and the pit in my stomach deepens. I shoot back a quick reply, pretending everything's fine.

> All good. See you soon.

But nothing feels good. My heart keeps racing as I keep glancing between the clock on my phone and the street. The Uber finally pulls onto the street next to the parking lot, and I rush over, throwing myself into the backseat, grateful to be out of the open. The driver greets me, but I barely acknowledge him, my mind spinning.

As the car pulls out of the lot, I steal one last glance at my car, sitting lopsided with its flat tire. For the first time, I realize I'm not just late for a meeting—I might be in real danger.

CHAPTER 16

CALL ME A FOOL, but I can't think of anyone else who could have done it besides Evelyn.

This feels too deliberate. The slashed tire, the timing—it makes little sense. Not in this neighborhood, not with my routine. This wasn't just a random act of vandalism. It feels like... a warning.

Evelyn has already done plenty; it wouldn't surprise me if she went above and beyond again. I was so stupid and naïve to break the news about this client to Evelyn last night.

Be a better person. Take the high road. Give her the benefit of the doubt.

I want to listen to Jenna, but look where it got me.

By the time I get home, I'm enraged.

I slam the front door behind me, fully expecting to get

some raised eyebrows. Sure enough, Evelyn is sitting at the kitchen island, sipping a glass of wine, as usual. She glances over her shoulder; her face scrunched in mild disapproval.

But I no longer care about her disapproval, nor do I care how she feels.

I trudge to the kitchen, facing her head-on. My voice comes out involuntarily. "Did you do it?"

My nostrils flare and my fists clench tightly. Evelyn stares at me in shock—her mouth hangs open, and terror fills her wide eyes. I must look terrifying.

"What are you talking about?"

"You slashed my tire, didn't you?"

"What?" She flaps her hand at her face, as if there's too much heat in the room. "What on earth do you mean?"

I point my index finger at her. "It's you, isn't it?" I scream at her from the top of my lungs; I just can't help it. Evelyn almost lost me another client today. I'm confident she's playing these games with me, but God knows why.

But tonight, we will get to the bottom of it.

Evelyn keeps staring at me, lost for words.

"Why did you slash my tire?"

She pitches her voice higher, "Don't be ridiculous. I didn't do shit."

But I'm not convinced. First the email, then my meds, and now my tire. What's next?

I'm terrified to find out.

"You need to be packing your shit soon and getting out of here, do you understand? I don't know what your motive is, or what you're doing, but ever since you've arrived, it's been HELL!"

And it's true: these four days have been nothing but a nightmare. All she has been doing is sabotaging me and making my life difficult. And none of it makes sense why.

"Are you saying I should go back home?" I sense the hurt in her voice.

"Yes, that's what I'm saying."

Jack walks down the stairs, and we both turn to look at him.

"Hey, ladies. What's going on here?" He looks confused and wary.

"Your wife..." I turn to look at her, only to see tears coming from her eyes. "Your wife wants me to leave."

She shakes her head and stands up to go get a tissue.

Are you kidding me? She's crying over our argument. What an actress!

Jack gazes at me and cocks his head, widening his eyes, as if waiting for me to explain. Evelyn is standing by the kitchen island and wiping her tears with the tissue, but I swear to God I see a smile in the corner of her eyes.

They're both staring at me and waiting for me to say something.

I gaze at Jack. "I found my tire slashed this morning, and I was almost late for the important meeting with my client."

I should have given him a heads up via text during the day, but I was too upset and absentminded. Besides, Jack has done little to smooth things over with Evelyn. I don't believe he's likely to be supportive now.

Evelyn turns to Jack and whimpers, "She thinks I had something to do with the tire being slashed."

Jack slumps his shoulders and looks at me. "Em." It's that voice of resignation, but he knows well I am right.

I place my hands on my hips and straighten myself. "I want your mom to leave tomorrow."

Evelyn gasps, turns around and walks to the living room. Jack steps closer, lowering his voice. "Emily, let's think straight for a moment. I get where you're coming from, but we can't just throw her out like this."

I bite back a retort, trying to hold on to what little patience I have left. "Jack, this isn't some random guest over-staying their welcome. She's...messing with me, with us. You don't see it, because she's not doing it to you."

He runs a hand through his hair, looking conflicted. "I know she's difficult, but..." he wants to say something else, but he halts. "The tire thing—Em, you're a hundred percent sure it's Evelyn who did it?"

I take a deep breath, steadying myself. "If not her, then

who else? It's not just the tire, Jack. It's everything. First, the weird email sent to my client. Then my prescription meds get moved around just to mess with my head. And now this. I'm telling you, it all started when she came. She's trying to —" My voice cracks, and I hate how vulnerable I sound. "She's trying to sabotage me, Jack."

Jack bites his lip and looks at me. "I don't know what to say anymore. Are you sure it's her?" He gazes over at Evelyn.

"That's what I'm trying to figure out!" I nearly scream, the frustration bubbling over. And it doesn't help that Evelyn can overhear the entire conversation. She's just sitting in the living room and sipping her wine, as if she's watching a reality show live. "But I'm telling you, I can't live like this anymore. She's turning everything upside down, and I've had enough."

He sighs heavily and rubs his eyes. "You know I don't want things to be like this. But...asking her to leave? That's a little extreme, don't you think? She's only been here four days."

Here's the rational and composed Jack I'm used to seeing. It doesn't matter that my life is going to shreds, as long as he makes everything logical and right, somehow.

But I'm not convinced.

"Exactly. And I can't take another three. You also said she was staying three days, tops. And she's still here!" I snap, my voice sharper than I intended. "Look, I get it. She's your mom. But she's not my responsibility, Jack. She's making me miserable, and it's affecting everything. I can't think, I can't sleep, I can't even breathe in my home without feeling like I'm being watched or manipulated."

Jack holds my gaze, his eyes softening. "I'll talk to her. Maybe she doesn't realize how much stress she's causing. I'll make sure she backs off, okay?"

I shake my head. "No. Talking isn't going to fix this. She needs to go. Before something else happens."

Jack's eyes brighten for a split second—a sparkle I haven't seen before.

He doesn't respond right away, just stands there, looking torn between his loyalty to me and his mother. I know he's trying to keep the peace, but this isn't a situation that can be solved with a simple heart-to-heart.

Behind him, I hear Evelyn sniffling from the living room, playing the victim, as usual. And I can't take it anymore.

"I mean it, Jack," I say, my voice low but firm. "Tomorrow. She leaves."

He looks at me for a long moment, and for the first time, I see a flicker of something in his eyes—doubt. Maybe even fear. And I wonder, just for a second, if he knows more than he's letting on.

But then he turns away, walking toward the living room,

and I'm left standing in the kitchen, staring at the empty space where he was.

'Evelyn, you heard Emily. You need to leave tomorrow. You got that?"

Evelyn's soft sobs echo from the next room, but I no longer care. Tomorrow, she's gone.

One way or another.

JACK HAS AGREED to talk with Evelyn once she's calmed down, and convince her to leave tomorrow.

I've reasoned things through with Jack, and he seems to get it. No hard feelings. Whether she did all those terrible things or it's just a weird coincidence, it no longer matters. It's time for her to leave us alone. For everyone's sake.

Once things settle down, Jack insists that the three of us keep the reservation at his favorite restaurant. He's cleared his calendar for the occasion, so we might as well go. It's the last opportunity to smooth things over with Evelyn and send her off home on a more positive note tomorrow.

I agree with some hesitation, but quickly realize it's better than the alternative—staying in the house, simmering over the incident. At least at the restaurant, it's easier to act civil, or at least pretend to. In several hours, Evelyn will be sitting on the plane, hopefully realizing that her behavior hasn't made a wedge between Jack and me. We still stand on solid ground, albeit a little shaky.

Jack plasters on a smile as we arrive at the restaurant. It's always been his favorite. He's the type who enjoys the finer things in life: good food, fine wine, and high-end fashion. A metrosexual through and through, he can't live without his Gucci and Brioni clothing. As a corporate lawyer, he's always impeccably groomed—clean-shaven and smelling of cologne. He exudes confidence, and more than once, he's made it clear that he believes his opinions carry more weight than anyone else's.

In various social circles, Jack has been a guy to admire, despite his current lack of friendships. Over the years, he has worked hard to build up this new image and erase the old one.

I'm familiar with Jack's past, but I've never truly understood the depth of it, nor how he grew up. He's never shared what happened between him and his mom, or why their relationship is the way it is. All I know is that they lived alone after his father left his mother for a much younger woman.

I plan to ask during dinner. It's my last chance before Evelyn gets on the plane and waves us goodbye.

While seated at the table, Evelyn looks around and studies the room. The restaurant is one of those places where the second you step inside, you feel you need to stand up straighter. Everything about it oozes luxury, from the soft, ambient lighting to the rich mahogany furniture polished to perfection. You can smell the money before you even see the menu. In fact, the menu doesn't have any prices listed, so you know what kind of place this is. Jack has always believed it suits us well.

Evelyn seems to adore the place. Crisp white tablecloths cover each table, so immaculate they almost seem too perfect to touch. Evelyn takes the fabric between her fingers and rubs it, as if it's made of platinum.

"This place looks fabulous." Evelyn looks awestruck. Her eyes squint as she bites her lip. "Aren't you two a fancy bunch?"

"Well," Jack says as he gives me a quick gaze, "I think we all deserve to treat ourselves, don't we?"

Evelyn chuckles loudly, then snorts through her nose. This is all a game, and we all pretend everything is fine.

Fancy restaurants like this one only mean dinners take longer. Jack orders a bottle of wine while Evelyn and I check out the menus, flipping them over again and again. Awkward silence settles at the table, but it gives me a chance to gather my wits before I start with questions. After the waiter comes to collect our orders and menus, I put my glass up in the air and say cheers. Jack and Evelyn follow and raise their glass. Everything feels different. The mood has shifted, and it feels like we are one happy family.

"So," I place my elbows on the table and interlace my fingers, setting my eyes on my mother-in-law, "I'm dying to hear what Jack was like when he was a baby."

Evelyn's face turns pale instantly. She gazes at Jack, then fidgets in her seat.

"Well..." Evelyn finally finds her voice, "Jack was a wonderful boy."

She places her hand on her mouth and coughs.

I gaze at Jack, and he's staring at his wineglass.

Evelyn stops coughing and continues, "Let me tell you. Jack was one of the most curious boys you'd ever meet. All the kids in the neighborhood loved him. They were constantly looking out for him, knocking on our doors and begging to play with him. Back then, it was so much easier to let your child play in the open. Times have definitely changed."

Evelyn talks fast and doesn't look at me or Jack. It's almost like she's nervous or holding a secret she's afraid will slip out. A chill runs down my spine. Did something happen in Jack's childhood that Evelyn doesn't want to reveal? I can't help but feel a little excited. I get to learn more about Jack.

"Where did you guys live? A house?"

"Yes. It was a small bungalow in the Portland suburb. Wonderful little family town."

Things suddenly don't add up. I crease my brows and cock my head. "Wait. I thought Jack grew up in Seattle?"

My eyes dart between Jack and Evelyn, both still fidgeting in their seat.

"Oh," Evelyn gasps, "we did live in the Seattle area, but the first five years of Jack's life, we lived in Portland." She looks down and scratches her nose. "We moved to Seattle for my new job."

Jack looks at me and gives me a small smile before he diverts his gaze.

"I see. And what did you do?"

"Me?" Evelyn places her hand on her chest as if I am scolding her, and she tries to defend herself. "Well, I...I was a nanny for a nice family in Seattle, but then I decided to study law. So, I went to law school, got my degree, and got a job as a city clerk until I passed the bar."

Little nuggets of information about my mother-in-law. I'm loving this.

I had no idea she was a lawyer, too. But it makes sense—Jack was probably inspired by her and decided to follow in her footsteps.

"Oh, you're a lawyer?" I can't hide the surprise in my voice. "What type?"

"An immigration lawyer," she replied quickly.

But this still doesn't answer the key question: why is their relationship so estranged? I don't sense an ounce of love between them. I have little time to find out, and there are no guarantees I will tonight.

"So, tell me more about Jack," I press, my voice soft but persistent.

Evelyn's fingers tighten around the stem of her glass, knuckles turning white as if holding on to something fragile. She hesitates, glancing at Jack, whose gaze remains glued to his untouched wine. The tension between them could slice through the air.

"He was...a good boy," she repeats, almost too quickly, her words rehearsed. "Smart, quiet, always in his own little world. He had this way about him, you know? A way of thinking differently from other kids. Very independent."

Jack shifts uncomfortably in his seat, the leather squeaking under him, still refusing to meet my eyes. I study him, the confident man I've always known suddenly reduced to a shell, as if something unspeakable lurks just beneath the surface.

"Independent?" I prod. "How so?"

Evelyn forces a smile. "He didn't need much attention. Unlike other children, who always craved it, Jack was...self-sufficient."

Jack finally lifts his head, his eyes meeting mine for the briefest moment, before darting away again. His jaw clenches, and I can see the tension coiling tighter within him. Something is wrong, and I'm done tiptoeing around it.

"Is that why you two drifted apart?" I ask, my voice low but pointed. "Because Jack didn't need you?"

Evelyn flinches. Jack's head snaps up, and he opens his mouth as if to speak, but no words come out. Instead, he takes a long, deliberate sip of his wine, draining the glass in one go. The silence that follows is deafening.

"We didn't drift apart," Evelyn says, her voice wavering. "Life just...happened. Things got complicated."

"Well," I say, breaking the silence, "I hope whatever it was, it's in the past now. Because Jack deserves to be happy. We both do."

Evelyn stands up and goes to the bathroom, leaving Jack and me alone. As soon as Evelyn is out of earshot, I turn to Jack, "What's this all about?"

"What?" he says incredulously.

"You and your mom. You both look like a deer in a headlight. Is it something I've said or asked?"

Jack shakes his head. "Emily." He rubs his left eye with two fingers and runs them down his nose. An exasperated sigh comes out.

"What, Jack, what is it?" I'm growing impatient.

He scans his surroundings, a flicker of anxiety in his eyes, before his gaze snaps back to me. "Listen, I've been meaning to tell you something."

My stomach feels like something just dropped, taking my breath away. I stare at Jack, holding onto the table just in case. But just as Jack is about to confess whatever is on his mind, our waiter approaches our table, all chirpy, oblivious to the fact he's interrupted by something important.

"How's everything, folks? Can I get you more wine?"

Jack looks at me, then our glasses, almost empty. "Sure."

"All right. I'll be right back with your wine."

As the waiter finishes refilling our water glasses, Evelyn is shuffling her way back between the tables. She has a fresh layer of lipstick on, and she looks like she has gathered wits about her.

I roll my eyes. For fuck's sake. The moment's gone, and whatever Jack wanted to say stays unsaid. Still, I have a feeling I know what he was going to tell me, though I can't quite piece together how any of it connects to his mom.

CHAPTER 18

WHEN WE GET HOME, I tell them I'm going upstairs to take a shower.

Just knowing that Evelyn will be gone tomorrow makes everything feel lighter and easier. In retrospect, dinner was a great idea, because, when we get home, the tension has loosened.

Evelyn and Jack stay behind in the living room, a deep silence settling in.

When I reach the third floor, I open the bedroom door and shut it firmly, making enough noise to be heard downstairs. Then I tiptoe to the stairway and sit on the top step. Sounds travel easily in the house, but the distance to the living room isn't insignificant, so I strain to listen and wait.

There's some commotion in the kitchen, as if one of them

is moving dishes around, then I hear the cork pop out of a bottle. Then Jack's voice.

"Are you having more wine?" His voice is curt. Unkind.

"Yes, why? What's it to you?" Evelyn's voice is mocking.

"You've been helping yourself like you own the house. Don't you think it's rude to just take things without asking?"

Whoa! Jack is finally putting his foot down. Good for him.

Evelyn laughs. "Oh, please, Jack. You're telling me about things being taken without asking first? I guess I've learned from the best." Her words follow her deep, hearty laughter.

I hear steps from high heels, then they halt. I picture Evelyn walking across the floor to her favorite chair, plopping down, crossing her legs and sipping her wine.

"You're leaving tomorrow, right? Have you changed your flight yet?" Jack continues.

Silence.

"Talk to me, for God's sakes." Jack grows frustrated. He's whispering loudly, as if he knows someone might be listening in.

"You can't make me, Jack. I'm not leaving until we're squared away," says Evelyn. She sounds confident.

"Listen. It is not going to happen." I can imagine Jack's jaw clenched and his cheeks flushing with anger.

"Have you told your wife yet?" Evelyn's mocking voice persists.

"Stop it, damn it. There's nothing to tell."

"Is that right, Jack? Let me remind you. If it wasn't for me, you'd be rotting in prison now." Evelyn's voice is firm.

I gasp and immediately draw my hand to my mouth. Oh my God, what else has Jack done? Why would he go to jail? What kind of sacrifice did his mother make to protect him? Maybe I have underestimated her all along, and maybe she is just trying to repair their past. But if that's the case, why did she try to make my life miserable?

Nothing makes sense.

"You're delusional," Jack says. "In any case, I'd better see you out the door first thing in the morning, or there will be consequences. Do you understand?"

Evelyn says nothing in return. Only a little laugh follows.

"If you don't leave tomorrow, you will regret it. I'm dead serious."

Evelyn's voice drops. "You still owe me, Jack. Don't forget that."

Jack's reply is muffled, but I hear the sharp edge in his tone. "I've given you more than enough."

Seconds later, Jack stomps up the stairs. I stand up quickly, stomping into our bedroom, and slowly open and close the door. I sit on the bed, pretending to read the news on my phone, but I'm shaken. The conversation downstairs has chilled me to my core, and I can't un-hear it. A can of worms is now wide open.

Jack looks agitated when he comes upstairs. He doesn't even look at me as he walks past and runs to the bathroom. He slams the door behind him, and seconds later, I hear a loud noise as if something got dropped and hit the floor.

"Are you okay?" I yell out loud enough for Jack to hear me.

"Yeah."

I want to ask him about what he was going to say at dinner tonight, but perhaps it's not the best time. He's obviously shaken by the conversation with Evelyn and I'm....well, I'm riddled with questions what his mother meant.

It's all as clear as mud. I don't know what to think anymore. On the one hand, I find relief in the fact Jack is not on Evelyn's side; on the other, I'm concerned about the secrets they're both harboring like an amulet.

Jack comes out of the bathroom and trots to the bed. He looks ready to punch something.

"Hey."

"Hey," he responds without looking at me. His back is turned to me while he takes his clothes off, ready to go to bed.

"Did you have a nice evening?"

Jack stays quiet until he sits on the bed to take his socks off. "Not bad. You?"

"Yeah, not bad. It was nice talking to Evelyn and learning more about you." I observe Jack's moves. He shakes his head as if bothered by the entire ordeal.

"I hope it will make you happy to know that she's going home tomorrow."

After listening to their conversation, I am not so sure. "Oh. She is?"

"Yes. She's getting on a flight tomorrow." He finally looks at me. "It's what you wanted. Right, Emily?"

Well, we both want it, but I don't say anything.

"I think it's time for us to be alone. Ever since she arrived, things have been strange, don't you think?" I say.

He nods. "Yeah. Yeah. Did you say goodbye to her?"

"I'll do it in the morning."

Jack sits next to me on the bed, his shoulders slumped, as if he's carrying a heavy burden. I rest my hand on his back, feeling the tension in his muscles. He doesn't flinch, but he doesn't relax, either.

"Are you okay?" I ask softly, trying to sound like I'm just concerned about his mood, not digging for details.

"Yeah, just tired," he says, his voice flat, distant.

We sit in silence for a moment; our secrets are pushing a wedge between us. I don't know what's worse—what I overheard or the fact that I can't ask him about it. Not yet, anyway. Jack stands up and walks to the window, looking out into the darkness. The city is quiet at this time of night.

"I'll make sure she's gone in the morning," he says, almost to himself.

I swallow hard, wondering if that's a promise or a threat.

"Okay."

Jack turns back to me, his face still etched with anger and concern. He's always been hard to read, but tonight, he feels like a stranger.

"Let's get some sleep," he says, pulling the covers back and slipping into bed. I follow, but sleep is the furthest thing from my mind. As I lie next to him, I can hear his breathing slowly, feel the warmth of his body beside mine, but my thoughts are miles away.

I've wanted Evelyn to leave so badly. But after hearing Jack's conversation with her, I can't help but wonder—why does *he* want her gone, too?

CHAPTER 19

JUST WHEN YOU think it can't get any worse, it does.

The following morning, I'm in the kitchen, making coffee, when I hear a strange sound. It's almost as if I'm in a cave, and water droplets have fallen into a pool of water, making a loud echo.

Something seems wrong.

I gaze at the ceiling above the kitchen and dart my eyes along the edge until I spot water dripping from the ceiling. My hand automatically moves to my mouth. "Oh, my God."

There has to be a flood coming from Evelyn's bathroom.

I look closer, and the ceiling has begun to warp and sag under the weight of the accumulating water. Small, discolored patches spread, slowly darkening as the dampness seeped through. Thin cracks have formed spider-webbing across the plaster, while droplets gathered at the edges of the cracks, trembling before releasing in slow, uneven drips. Each drop splashes onto the floor below with a faint but persistent plop, leaving behind tiny, shimmering puddles.

"Jack!" I scream at the top of my lungs. "Jaaaack!"

The bedroom door upstairs opens, and Jack rushes down.

"What is it?" Jack is standing in the middle of the living room, only wearing his underwear.

I point at the ceiling, speechless and horrified.

Jack looks up, and his face pales. For a split second, we stand there, frozen, watching the water slowly claim the ceiling, its slow destruction filling the silence with dread.

"Damn it," Jack mutters, rushing toward the stairs. "It's coming from Evelyn's room. I'll check it out."

He takes two steps a time, and I hear him pound on the door. "Evelyn! Open up!" His voice is strained, panicked.

No answer.

"Evelyn!" He bangs harder, and I can hear the doorknob rattle.

My heart races as I stand shaking in the kitchen. My hands tremble as I think of what could have happened. Is Evelyn hurt? Did something happen during the night? My mind spirals, filling with worst-case scenarios. I grab my phone off the counter, ready to call for help, but I hesitate. Jack hasn't called out for me yet.

A loud crash snaps me out of my thoughts. Jack must have forced the door open.

"Emily!" His voice is sharp, desperate.

I race up the stairs, my feet pounding against the hardwood floor. When I reach Evelyn's room, I'm met with a sight I wasn't prepared for.

Water is gushing from the tub faucet, pooling onto the floor, and there, lying just inside the doorframe, is Evelyn. She's motionless, face down on the tiles, her clothes soaked through. The water runs around her like she's part of the flood itself.

I gasp, clamping my hand over my mouth once again. "Oh, my God... is she—?" I run to the faucet and shut it down to lessen damage. The bathroom looks like a swimming pool, with water gushing from all directions, spilling from the edge of the tub. It's a terrible sight.

Jack kneels beside her, his hands hovering over her as if unsure whether or not to touch her. "She's breathing," he says quickly. "But she must've slipped..."

I inch closer, my eyes wide with fear and confusion. "What should we do?"

Evelyn's face is pale, her body limp, as if all the energy has drained out of her. Her face, usually sharp with judgment, is now dull and unfocused. She looks smaller somehow, fragile, as though whatever fire once burned inside her has been extinguished. The sight of her like this unsettles me

—her immobility is a stark contrast to the domineering presence she's always carried.

Jack moves swiftly, his expression hardening as he lifts Evelyn's limp body into his arms, water dripping from her as he carries her to the bed. I watch, my heart pounding in my chest, as he checks her pulse again. "She's still out cold. I'll call an ambulance."

I turn on my heels, ready to dash out of the room and grab my phone, when the sudden force pulls me back. Jack has grabbed my hand and looks me in the eye. "No, Emily. You're not calling anybody."

Their last night's conversation crosses my mind. This accident suddenly seems like more than just a coincidence.

I swallow, trying to process what Jack means. My mind races. Their cryptic conversation from last night echoes in my head.

If it wasn't for me, you'd be rotting in prison now.

I'd better see you out the door first thing in the morning, or there will be consequences.

And as I stare at Jack, I realize I don't know what's more terrifying—the water spilling into the house, or the secrets about to spill into the light.

CHAPTER 20

THE CHILL in the air is palpable. It feels like Jack and I are trying to get away with murder. Evelyn is lying in bed; her limp and pale body remains motionless.

I look up at Jack. "What should we do?"

Call me the worst person in the whole wide world, but in this moment, I'm more concerned about Evelyn's inevitable extended stay at our home than her well-being.

Jack shrugs. "I'm sure she'll be fine. She is just unconscious, but she's breathing okay."

We stare at her and watch her chest rise and descend.

"How do you think she fell?"

Jack shrugs his shoulders. "No idea."

"She must have fallen after she turned the faucet, obviously." I say, feeling like a moron. Isn't it too obvious to even say out loud?

"Of course she did," Jack roars. "She had five million glasses of wine last night, for crying out loud. She probably fell to the floor, hammered."

Sounds about right.

"Do you think I should change her clothes?" I ask. "She's completely soaked, plus she's going to ruin the mattress."

Jack nods quickly. "I think that's a good idea."

We both gaze at her suitcase on the floor. Jack walks to it and opens it up. Her stuff is still inside. He rummages through the luggage until he finds a red dress with flowers on it. He turns to me while holding it. "This one?"

"Sure." We approach the bed and watch Evelyn, unsure of ourselves. "Do you want me to undress her?" I offer.

"Okay. Yes. That'd be great."

The wet clothes are so stuck to her skin, it takes a while to peel them off her body. She's by no means a heavy woman, but in this state, she feels like a whale.

Evelyn is now lying completely naked.

"Does she have more underwear?" I inquire.

While looking for dry underwear, Jack unearths something from her luggage. It's a wrapped-up gift, a small box. It must be our wedding gift that Evelyn alluded to when she first arrived. She wanted to find a perfect occasion to give it to us, except that occasion hasn't materialized yet.

Jack holds it delicately in his hands. He places it near his ear and shakes it lightly, but the content inside is safely packaged and doesn't rattle.

"Should we open it?" The curiosity gets the better of me.

Jack shrugs. "I guess. Not like she would care."

This feels so heartless—opening the gift—but the good news is that Evelyn is just passed out, lost in her drunken state. She'll be fine and probably won't mind that we opened it. Finally.

Jack hesitates, but then proceeds to tear the gift wrap until it's completely stripped. He opens the box and pulls out a strange object: a vintage, broken clock that has seen its days.

Jack turns it over and over in his hands, studying it. "Hmmm. Strange."

I scrunch my nose. "What the hell is that? Why would she give us a broken clock?"

Jack shrugs again. "Beats me."

He seems indifferent, but I'm disturbed by the gift—it seems more like a provocation than a kind gesture. What does a broken clock mean to Evelyn?

Jack rummages through the luggage again until he finds a new pair of underwear. It's granny-style, which surprises me. I'd expected Evelyn to wear something foxier, given her personality.

But then, something else strikes me as strange. The room

freezes as the realization hits me. "Hey, Jack." My voice is barely a whisper.

"What?"

"Your mom...I don't see any scars from her heart surgery."

Jack throws his arms up in the air. "Oh, for God's sakes, Emily, are you serious right now? How could you worry about that shit? We've got bigger issues to deal with, don't you think?"

I gaze at Jack, looking pissed at my inquiry. "Okay, fine." I let it go for now.

We dress Evelyn with difficulty, and march out of the room to inspect the damage. Downstairs, the house looks like it has seen better days. Of all things we have to deal with, fixing up the place somehow becomes our top priority.

"Oh, God. We should call someone right away before the floors collapse." I plead with Jack.

"I'll take care of it all. Don't worry."

"Are you sure?" I ask, feeling bad that I'd prefer to go to work than deal with all this shit.

"Yes," Jack repeats.

I stand there, hesitant to move, but I proceed. If Jack says he will take care of everything, then so be it.

I leave the house for work, because, frankly, I can't deal with this right now. I grab my bag, the keys, and give Jack one last glance before stepping out the door. He's still inspecting the ceilings, his brow furrowed, as if calculating his next move.

The cool morning air hits my face as I step outside, and I take a deep breath, trying to clear my head. On my way to the office, I notice how smooth the drive feels now that the tire's been fixed. At least one thing in my life is back in order, even if everything else is falling apart.

But even as I drive, my thoughts are clouded by the scene I've just left behind. Evelyn's limp body, the water pooling around her, Jack's calculated responses...none of it feels right. It's unsettling, but I push it aside. I have to get through the day.

At the office, I sit at my desk, mindlessly going through emails, but my focus is shot. All I can think about is the morning. The sound of water dripping. The way Jack shrugged off Evelyn's fall. She'll be fine. His words replay in my mind.

What if she isn't?

At noon, I'm back with my therapist. I sit across from Dr. Whitman again, her calm, ever-composed face staring back at me. She has her leg crossed, violently rocking her hanging one.

"So, Emily, do you remember we said I'd see you tomorrow, and not today?"

"Oh." I clutch my phone and tug at the case nervously.

"Today is only Thursday. I can only imagine you've been distressed and forgot the timing of our appointment."

I shake my head, surprised to hear I've mixed up the days. But I'm almost a hundred percent sure Dr. Whitman scheduled a session for today. I'd even put it on my calendar as a reminder, like I always do. "Sorry, Dr. Whitman." I get ready to stand up and leave. "Should I come back tomorrow?"

"Sit down," she says. "My noon slot got canceled, so we're good. I guess you don't need to come back tomorrow unless you really want to."

"Right." I nod, although I'm petrified. I think Dr. Whitman is playing with my mind.

I've been off my game, but she doesn't even know half of it. Everything is crashing around me, and I'm doing my best to survive.

I've been coming here for over a year now, but this time, the session feels different. The weight on my chest is heavier than before. My thoughts are more scattered. My heart feels like it's constantly racing.

"It's been...hard," I say, trying to gather my words. "As I said before, Jack's mom is here, and it's like everything is falling apart."

Dr. Whitman leans forward, her eyes searching mine. "Falling apart how?"

I shake my head. "She's... weird. I don't know how else to

describe it. She's too comfortable here. It's like she knows more than I do about my life. And Jack... he's not the same. He's distant. Secretive. I don't know what's going on with him."

Dr. Whitman doesn't respond right away. She tilts her head, her voice soft and neutral. "Do you think you're over-thinking things? Could it be the stress of the honeymoon, the new marriage, and adjusting to his mother being around?"

My pulse quickens. "That's the thing—I don't know anymore. I feel like I'm losing it, but at the same time, I can't shake the feeling that something is really, really wrong."

My home: it feels like a sandcastle crashing against the turbulent sea. It took some time to build, but vanished within seconds. But I won't let Evelyn ruin it all. There are some sand specks left of the castle that can be salvaged.

Just as I think there is hope, Dr. Whitman leans forward and pauses before asking, "Do you trust Jack?"

CHAPTER 21

Jack

"FUCK." It's the only word I can muster as I stare at the warped ceiling.

Ever since we moved to the townhouse—or, as Emily and I jokingly call it, the Mr. and Mrs. Ross Residence—we have had no major issues, like plumbing or electrics or the roof. The previous owners upgraded the place from top to bottom, so when we put an offer on it, it was a turnkey. I don't even know who to call.

Emily's departure from the house is confirmed when the front door slams. Relief washes over me. She's one less thing to worry about.

I need to handle the situation delicately, but I first need to find someone to repair all the damage. The ceiling looks as if it's about to collapse, and the wood on the second floor is soaked and protruding. That stale air that a flood brings is creeping in and settling between the walls. No doubt it will all take a while to restore everything to its original state.

Even as the issue with the house mounts, it's still the least of my problems right now.

Evelyn.

What the hell do I do with her? After everything we've been through, she'd still had the audacity to send me threatening texts after our conversation last night, warning that she'd spill everything to Emily if I didn't do her a favor. And if that wasn't bad enough, she'd given me a deadline. I had until the end of the week to carry out the misdeed. And that terrifies me. How am I going to pull it off with only two days left in the week?

I only hope to God Emily doesn't suspect any of it. She's been more inquisitive lately, as if she knows there is a secret, but I can't let her in on it. Not yet. And maybe, with some luck, Evelyn will change her mind—if she ever wakes up.

I go upstairs to check up on her.

I circle around her bed, like a shark, and watch her carefully. Her breathing is consistent. Her hands are resting crossed on her chest. If it wasn't for breathing, I'd think she was deceased. Her calm is unnerving, and I wonder if and when she will wake up.

Under the bed, I spot the knife I'd used to slash Emily's

tire. I'd hoped she would find it—given how much of a snoop she is—but she didn't. My plan to sabotage her and pin everything on Evelyn, making her the scapegoat, had worked. Hard evidence would have solidified Emily's suspicions, but it doesn't matter now.

I thought I could just carry on after sending that email to Emily's client and hiding her meds. The consequences would've been too obvious not to trigger something—push her over the edge, make her doubt herself, pin it all on Evelyn and make them true enemies. But the plan to get Evelyn to leave tomorrow would've been good enough on its own, and would have worked perfectly if it wasn't for the fall. Now everything's more complicated, and I don't know how much longer I can keep this under control.

Before I go downstairs to look for a repairman, I approach Evelyn's bed to take one last look. She looks pale, as if all the blood has drained from her body. She was a beauty back in the day. I mean, she's not ugly now, but she hasn't aged as well as she could have. I remember when she was into running marathons and swimming twenty laps in an Olympic-sized pool every day. Her triathlon training was rigorous and demanding, but she could keep up. But now, she's not in best shape, and wrinkles have formed around her eyes and lips.

Evelyn is the person who fights with all her might. I'm

sure she will bounce back soon. I sure as hell hope I won't be around to see it.

I hover over her body and shake my head. "Oh, Evelyn. You're a fool if you think you could outsmart me." I chuckle. "You're something else if you think you can just come to my home unannounced."

The question that's been nagging me is: how did Evelyn find out where we live? We've only been in this house for less than a year, and our address isn't tied to our names or listed publicly. Someone—or something—must have tipped her off. But knowing Evelyn, with her lawyer's cunning, she's resourceful enough to dig up anything.

When someone really wants to find you, they will—no matter the cost. When I asked how she found us, she just gave me that infamous, guttural laugh that sends shivers down my spine.

I size her up and down while my mind races. At the least, she's not dangerous while she's unconscious, thank goodness. But what happens when she regains her consciousness and becomes belligerent all over again?

I gather my wits and firm up the plans in my head. First, the house needs to be fixed up before everything crashes. Second, I need to get rid of Evelyn as soon as possible. I must send her off home and find a way never to see her again.

I take one last look before heading downstairs when, suddenly, Evelyn's eyes snap open, like a cork exploding from a bottle. A slow, sardonic smile spreads across her face as she locks eyes with me, her gaze sharp and menacing, like daggers cutting through the air.

She laughs. "You call me a fool, Jack?"

She swings her legs to the side of the bed and stands up. Now, we're standing face-to-face, her head positioned a lot lower than mine.

"You look surprised, Jack. Unfortunately for you, I'm intact and feeling quite good."

My blood is boiling and my face crunches with anger. I'd forgotten how crafty Evelyn can be. She's been acting this whole time.

"What the hell do you think you're doing?" I ask through clenched teeth. She's a total psycho if she's gone so far as to fake her own downfall.

"I'm doing fine, thank you very much." She smiles sarcastically.

"Ugh. What the hell?"

"Jack." She's right up in my face now. "All you have to do is one favor, and you're off the hook. You owe me, Jack."

"Listen, lady, I don't owe you shit. And I think you need to pack your stuff and leave. Now!" I shout in her face and point my finger toward the door.

Evelyn doesn't budge.

Her stupid smile hasn't left her face, and she keeps staring at me, clearly enjoying my reaction.

"When are you going to tell your wife what you did? Huh? Don't you think she deserves to know?"

"Leave my wife out of this." Evelyn knows my only goal is to keep my biggest secret from Emily. Evelyn's played me like a fiddle and knows she holds a royal flush in her hands.

She walks by and brushes her shoulder against me. I hate how provocative she is, and how, like always, she gets on my nerves. She stops at the top of the stairs and turns around to look at me. The smile on her face disappears, and she looks angry more than anything.

"All I ask is that you do me this favor in exchange for my help years ago. It's the least you can do."

"Listen. I can't. I can't do it. I'm going to lose my bar license."

I trudge toward her, our eyes locked.

"If you don't do me the favor, I'm telling your wife everything you did. And she will kick you to the curb the second she finds out what you are."

I cock my head at her and squint my eyes. "Is that a threat?"

I'm standing so close to Evelyn, I can feel her breathing. She's silent, as if contemplating her next words. She's the kind of person who crawls into your skin and gets stuck. Getting rid of her takes a Herculean effort.

"It's not a threat, Jack. It's a fact."

In that moment, something snaps inside me. Without

thinking, I lift my arm and shove Evelyn hard, watching as she tumbles down the stairs. My hands fly to my mouth in shock, my eyes locked on the horrifying scene unfolding before me, barely able to process what I've just done.

The tumbling sound echoes through the house, and to my ears, it seems like an endless charade. Time passes in slow motion when, finally, Evelyn's body halts at the bottom of the stairs.

She's lying in an awkward position: one of her arms is behind her back, her legs are twisted at unnatural angles, and her head is turned slightly to the side, resting against the floor. For a moment, there's nothing but eerie silence. The air feels thick, suffocating, as I stand frozen at the top of the stairs, my heart hammering in my chest.

I don't know how long I stare at her lifeless form before I finally move, my body on autopilot, descending the stairs slowly. With every step, my breath comes in shallow gasps. I kneel next to her, reaching out a trembling hand to check if she's still breathing.

She is, but barely. A weak rise and fall of her chest are the only sign of life. I should feel relief, but all I can think about is what I've done. I push the guilt down, telling myself it was an accident, that she provoked me. I didn't mean for this to happen.

But the truth gnaws at me.

I pull out my phone to call for help, my thumb hovering

over the screen. Then I hesitate. If Evelyn wakes up, what will she say? Will she tell the truth that I pushed her? Or will she keep quiet?

I can't take that chance.

I slip the phone back into my pocket and stare down at her again. "Hey, are you okay?" I whisper, as if talking to her will somehow make everything better.

Of course, there is no peep coming out of Evelyn. I don't expect it. This time, she's not pretending to be hurt. This time, she looks completely fucking mangled.

CHAPTER 22

Emily

BY LUNCHTIME, I'm tempted to call Jack and check in, but something stops me. Maybe it's the guilt that I left the house this morning and let Jack handle everything. Or maybe it's the fear of what he'll say. Instead, I bury myself in work, hoping it will distract me.

But as the hours pass, that uneasy feeling grows, gnawing at the back of my mind. What if Jack didn't call for help? What if there's more to this than an accident?

Can you trust Jack?

Dr. Whitman's words echo in my mind. The truth is, so much has happened since Evelyn arrived, I don't even know if I can trust myself.

When the workday finally ends, I drive home, my stomach in knots. The house looks the same from the outside —calm, ordinary. But when I step inside, the tension is thick, and I'm perturbed by the deep silence.

I walk in, tripping over my steps, as anxiety and anticipation overpower me. The house is dark and spooky, and the blinds in the living room are shut, making the apartment feel like a coffin. Jack must have done this, but why? We love natural light coming in through the window, especially in the afternoon before the city descends into complete darkness.

I yell out my usual hello, my voice cracking. It's an old habit I can't break ever since Jack and I moved in together. I hear hello back coming from the kitchen, but the tone is monotonous and unexciting.

I find Jack in the kitchen, cleaning up the water damage. His face is unreadable, focused. I glance around, searching for any sign of Evelyn. Not here.

"She's upstairs," Jack says without looking up, as if he knows what I'm thinking. "Resting."

I nod, unsure of what to say. "Did you...call anyone?"

"I handled it," he replies, his tone curt.

Something in his voice makes my skin prickle. "Is she okay?"

"She'll be fine," he says again, wiping down the counter, then his forehead with the back of his arm. "Nothing to worry about."

Jack is elusive and doesn't answer my question. I raise my voice. "Did you call for help or not, Jack?"

He stops what he is doing and looks at me. "Stop fucking yelling at me, Emily. Don't you see I'm busy cleaning this shit up?"

"I wasn't yelling. I need to know if Evelyn is getting help. How much longer is she going to be around?"

He shakes his head and throws his arms up in the air. "I don't fucking know, Emily! Whatever it takes for a person to recover, okay?"

Maybe now is the time to ask about her heart surgery—wouldn't she be in much worse shape if she'd just had a major operation? And I saw no evidence of it when we changed her this morning. But Jack seems in a foul mood, so I doubt he'll be explaining anything.

I sniff and smell something strange—a mix of fire smoke and something metallic, like burning wires or scorched metal. My stomach tightens with unease as I scan the room, trying to pinpoint the source of the unsettling scent.

"What's that smell?"

"What smell?" Jack says.

"I don't know—it smells like something burned, mixed with blood."

"Gosh, you're imagining things again, Emily."

I wave my hand and walk away. I can't deal with Jack right now.

Jack finishes cleaning up and makes a beeline for the living room.

"I'm going to check up on her, okay?" I say.

I size him up and down, sensing the accumulated tension in his body. He just stares at me with his creased forehead, as if he's thinking hard.

"Are you okay?"

"Yeah, I am. It just...it took me forever to find someone to come in at a last minute. A guy named Peter and his crew are coming first thing tomorrow morning to work on the ceilings and floors."

"Good." I force a smile.

Jack oozes concern, but I'm still afraid to ask what's bothering him, except for the obvious. I've never seen him so rattled. He's always so calm and measured, and in control of a situation.

The place looks like a jungle. All the furniture that was affected by the flood was piled and covered with a tarp in the corner. The ceilings look like they belong to an abandoned building, battered and worn by the elements. The Mr. and Mrs. Ross Residence looks like a war zone.

I walk upstairs to check up on Evelyn. The wood feels funny under my feet, sending a series of sharp creaks through the otherwise quiet house.

Facing the helpless Evelyn is the last thing I want to do

after a long day at work, but I tell myself I have no choice. I need to assess her condition to see how long we're stuck with her in the house.

The door of her room is ajar. I slowly open it, my hands trembling, as I fear what awaits inside.

There's nothing unusual except for Evelyn lying in bed. She's in the same position I left her in this morning. Her skin looks as pale as ever, and her hair is disheveled. Her breathing looks more sporadic, as if some strange force pushes on her chest to move air in and out of her lungs.

I approach her bed, hovering over her motionless body. She looks unchanged at first glance, the same as she did earlier—except for one thing that strikes me as deeply odd.

A large purple bruise has bloomed across her left cheek, something I didn't notice this morning. My eyes dart down to her hands, where I spot another dark bruise, just as angry and swollen. They look painful, as if the fall had inflicted more damage than I initially realized. It's unnerving, the sight of it, like a silent scream etched across her skin. It's possible the bruising was delayed and only showed up later. But Jack had to have seen the bruises and didn't say anything. I guess maybe he wouldn't in his cranky state of mind.

I've never dealt with something like this before, but I'm certain Evelyn needs to be hospitalized. We can't keep her here any longer—it's not safe for her, and it's certainly not safe for us. If we can't ship her back to Seattle, then Boston General will have to do. Anywhere, as long as it's away from my home.

I'm desperate now. Desperate to get rid of Evelyn before things spiral further out of control.

CHAPTER 23

Emily

THAT EVENING, Jack and I go to bed, both exasperated by this new situation. The house is in shambles and God knows how much time and money it will take to repair all the damage. My mother-in-law is lying in bed in the guest room, and we don't know when she will wake up or be functional again. And the tension between Jack and me is bloating up like a balloon.

This can't be good.

As I suspect, Jack doesn't broach the subject, because the last twenty-four hours seem to have been too much for him. When he's under stress, Jack clams up and doesn't talk.

But we need to. We need to come up with the plan on what to do with Evelyn when she "wakes up."

I lie next to Jack in bed. He's staring at the ceiling with one of his arms resting on his forehead. He's clearly thinking. I need to find out what about.

"Hey, babe." We're usually affectionate in bed, but I don't dare touch him. "Can we talk about your mom?"

Jack glances at me, then returns to the original pose. "What about her?"

"Should we call the doctor? Take her to the hospital?"

Jack rolls his eyes but doesn't say anything.

"I mean, her state isn't normal at all. She hasn't woken up since she fell this morning. Right?"

Jack pauses, then says, "Right."

"She's still alive. I saw her breathing. But we don't know what's wrong with her." I pause. Jack still says nothing. "I've Googled to see what could be wrong, and I'm still not sure. From the symptoms, she could be in a coma. She could have had a stroke. If we don't get her into a hospital, her condition could get worse."

Jack peeps at me, his forehead creased from thinking. "I appreciate you looking into this, but let me worry about Evelyn, okay? I'll call a doctor tomorrow and see what we can do for her."

I sigh in relief. I'd feel terrible if Evelyn died in our guest room. "Yes, that sounds good."

"Are we ready to sleep?" Jack is quick and curt.

"Sure."

We turn our back to each other after we say goodnights. No usual kisses tonight.

Not surprisingly, I have a nightmare that night.

In my dream, the house is darker than usual; the walls creaking with an eerie groan, as though they're bending under the weight of something invisible. I'm standing at the bottom of the stairs, looking up. There's a shadow at the top, barely visible, but I know who it is.

Evelyn.

She stands still, her eyes fixed on me, unblinking. I try to move, to run up the stairs, to help her, but my legs feel like they're stuck in quicksand. No matter how hard I try, I can't move. Her lips curl into a strange smile, and then suddenly, she falls. I hear the sickening thud of her body hitting each step, but this time...this time, I'm the one at the top.

I wake up, startled, my heart racing. Jack's still beside me, fast asleep, breathing evenly. I glance at the alarm clock —it's 3:22 a.m. The house is quiet, unnervingly so. The dream clings to me, and I can't shake the feeling that something isn't right.

I tiptoe out of bed and quietly make my way to the guest room. I need to check on Evelyn, to assure myself that she's still there, still alive, that the dream was just my mind playing tricks on me.

The door creaks as I push it open, and I peer inside. Evelyn lies in the bed, as motionless as she's been since the fall. She's still breathing. But something feels off. There's a stillness in the room that's unnerving, like the air itself is waiting for something.

I glance down at her luggage on the floor, trying to determine if it's been moved. My memory has been unreliable since my own coma, so I can't be sure. It's maddening. Frustrated, I shake my head and head to the bathroom on autopilot, hoping to find some evidence. There's nothing. Absolutely nothing.

Maybe my mind is messing with me.

I back away slowly, closing the door just as carefully as I opened it, and retreat to the hallway.

Back in bed, I lie awake, staring at the ceiling, my thoughts whirling.

Do you trust Jack?

Things have become strange. I don't think I can trust anyone.

CHAPTER 24

Emily

PETER and his crew arrive early in the morning. It takes a while for them to haul in all of their tools and what-not, and I'm annoyed with the commotion this early. But I should feel relief. We have lucked out finding Peter on a whim, and the only way to hire him this quickly was to pay him the premium price. His service won't be cheap, that's for sure. But it's worth it. They will be working around the clock and hope to finish in a few days. At least, according to Jack.

Because I've been up since the wee hours, I'm already in the kitchen, staring at nothing while having my coffee. The dream last night had me awake half the night, making me reflect on everything that's happened with Evelyn.

Jack joins me in the kitchen and says good morning

without looking at me. He approaches the coffee machine and pours himself a cup. Between us, there's a deep and long silence, as if we're two strangers.

Peter walks down the stairs and stops in the living room, looking at both of us. "Hey, there's a person in the second-floor room."

He seems somewhat perplexed, as if he doesn't know what to do with this working condition.

Jack chimes in, "She's just resting. Go ahead and do what you have to."

"Oh-kay." Peter looks as if he has more questions but doesn't proceed raising them.

He goes back upstairs, and seconds later, we hear him talking to his guys, probably relaying Jack's message.

Jack's eyes are still avoiding me. But I move into his line of vision so he can't avoid me.

"Jack, you're calling a doctor today. Right?"

Jack bores his gaze into me, but his eyes seem hollow. "Yes, I already told you. Geez, Emily."

He gets aggravated so easily now. This is exactly what I've been worried about. I can only surmise that Evelyn's arrival into our life has everything to do with Jack's newly estranged behavior.

Out of desperation, I make a last-minute decision.

"Jack, I'll be home late tonight."

"Okay."

Jack doesn't ask why or what I'm going to do tonight. His lack of care worries me. But I say nothing and leave the kitchen to get ready for work.

I am planning dinner with Jenna tonight for two reasons. One, I don't want to come home to the newly created mess. And two, I need clarity about the Evelyn situation. Even if Jenna doesn't give solid advice, at least I'll have a chance to talk about it without being barked at.

Jenna seems to be worried about me. After I text her to ask if she is available tonight, she responds right away.

> Absolutely. I'll see you at 7, the usual place?

I will fly to the Moon if Jenna suggests it as our meeting placc.

My workday turns out to be unproductive. I'm so shaken by the happenings at home that I can't concentrate. I kill time by shopping on Amazon and reading emails. Some are urgent, but my mind is so scattered, I can't concentrate enough to respond.

I arrive early for my rendezvous with Jenna and order myself a strong Manhattan. It's not my usual choice of drink, but tonight, I need something stiff. I've told myself alcohol is not the way to manage my anxiety—but tell that to my brain. It's hard to reason with feelings, especially when they're on overdrive.

By the time Jenna arrives, I'm already a little buzzed. She saunters through the door and looks around, then down at her watch, realizing she's running late. I wave at her, and she hastens her steps, looking frazzled.

"I am so sorry. Traffic is awful." She rolls her eyes in annoyance.

"That's okay."

She slides her purse from her shoulder while seating herself in the booth across from me. "Are you okay?"

I gaze down at my drink. "You mean this?"

She laughs. "No."

I cut her off. "This is more than okay. Trust me." I give her a crooked smile.

Jenna laughs. She's probably about to order one of those herself.

"Wait, isn't tonight your tennis night?" I ask.

As long as I've known Jenna, she has gone to her tennis sessions with friends, and she wouldn't do anything to miss them.

She freezes. "Tennis?" She waves her hand at me. "Oh yeah. That...I canceled it tonight, because my wrist isn't feeling right."

"Oh, what's wrong with your wrist?"

She circles it around like she just discovered it. "I don't know. I was planning on seeing a doctor soon."

She gazes down to look at the menu, while I fidget in my seat, feeling uncomfortable with the situation. Since when has Jenna sacrificed tennis for me? But I won't complain. Not today, when I desperately need to talk.

"So, what's going on with you, girl?" She looks up. "I don't remember the last time you asked me out twice in a week."

"Brace yourself," I quip. "I may be moving in with you pretty soon."

I laugh, but she doesn't. Her face turns stony, but I sense curiosity projecting from her eyes. "Why? What's going on?"

I shake my head. "Oh, God." The drink is making my words slurry. But at least I'm feeling darn good.

I unleash on Jenna like she's my psychologist. As I tell her the story about the flood in the bathroom and my mother-in-law getting into some kind of coma, Jenna's face turns darker. She swallows hard and stares at me, wide-eyed. She clearly doesn't know what to say. I've caught her off guard, and that's quite unusual for Jenna.

She leans against the seat and grabs the edge of the table, as if she's about to fall. "Oh, gosh. That's awful. So, how is she doing now?"

I shrug my shoulders as if I don't care, but it's the alcohol taking the edge off. "Oh, you know. The same, I guess. Jack was supposed to call a doctor today, so we'll see what to do next."

I'm telling her all this as if I'm talking about the weather. But Jenna looks outright stiff and uncomfortable. She lifts her drink, a glass of Cabernet, and nearly downs it.

As she puts the wineglass on the table, she gazes to her left, scrunching up her face, then looks at me. "Something's totally off here. I can just feel it."

"Like what?"

"I think Jack is hiding something. You should find out what it is."

"Wait, what? You think he's hiding something?"

She nods. "Nothing seems right, Emily."

"What about Evelyn?"

She pauses and stares at me. "What about her?"

"Well, she's the one who came suddenly into our lives and fucked everything up." I laugh, but it's not funny.

"I don't know. I still think Jack is hiding something. You should dig deeper, my friend."

"How?"

"Maybe hire a private investigator. I don't know."

I blink, processing her suggestion. Hire a private investigator? The idea feels so absurd, like something out of a cheap detective novel. But then again, everything about this situation with Evelyn feels surreal.

"A private investigator?" I repeat, half-laughing, but Jenna remains dead serious. Her eyes are locked on mine, her lips tight.

"Yes, Emily," she says firmly, leaning closer. "Think about it. Evelyn showing up out of the blue, then conveniently slipping into some sort of coma? Something's fishy."

My buzz suddenly fades as the weight of her words sinks in.

"What do you think it might be?" I ask, trying to keep my voice steady. "Do you think Jack tried to kill his mom when he was younger or something?"

The alcohol has completely taken control of my mind. I can't think clearly. Though, in this moment, the idea isn't outside the realm of possibilities. Anything and everything rings true to me right now.

Jenna shrugs but doesn't back down. "I don't know. But I do know something's not right. You've felt it too, haven't you?"

I nod slowly. As much as I hate to admit it, I have. The way Evelyn wormed her way into our lives, her strange behavior, the tension that seems to hang over everything since she arrived—it's all been gnawing at me. Then Jack turning into this belligerent beast ever since Evelyn injured herself. I'd kept telling myself I was overreacting, that it was just stress from the wedding and adjusting to married life.

But now Jenna's words are pulling those buried doubts to the surface.

"Emily," she whispers, her voice cutting through the fog in my mind. "You have to trust your instincts. If something feels off, there's a reason."

I sit back, my stomach churning. My thoughts race, and suddenly, the room feels too small, too stifling. I glance at Jenna, her face concerned but determined. She's right. I can't ignore this any longer.

I take a deep breath and look up at her. "Okay," I say. "I'll think about it."

I don't know of any private investigators, but there's always Google.

Jenna nods, a small smile tugging at her lips. "That's all I'm asking. Just...keep your eyes open. And if you need help, you know where to find me."

I give her a weak smile in return, but my mind is already elsewhere.

As we sit in silence, my thoughts drift back to the brownstone and Jack.

What if there's something deeper going on—something else Jack's been hiding from me all this time?

I drain the rest of my drink, the alcohol no longer providing the comfort it did earlier. Instead, all I feel now is a creeping unease, a growing certainty that whatever Evelyn and Jack are hiding, it's worse than I ever imagined.

CHAPTER 25

Emily

PETER and his team have made significant progress in restoring our home. The furniture is still tucked in the corner, but the ceiling above is clear and looks new and dry.

I don't say my hello as usual when I come home from dinner with Jenna. Jack had texted me earlier to say he'd be staying late at work, and Evelyn, I assume, is still upstairs.

All the lights come on when I flip the switches in the hallway. It feels less lonely and spooky this way. I walk to the kitchen to get myself a glass of water. After the Manhattans, I feel woozy and parched. I walk by the staircase, and I do a double take when I see a figure standing at the top, staring down at me.

Evelyn.

I gasp and jump back in fear, then rub my eyes to ensure it's not the effect of alcohol that makes me see things. But when I open my eyes, the figure is no longer there.

"Shit," I whisper to myself.

I trudge upstairs, my heart thumping in my chest. I have to see for myself.

As the floor under my feet creaks, I listen for any sounds from upstairs that would reveal any movement. Maybe Evelyn is fine and has been pretending this whole time?

When I reach the door of the guest room, I tiptoe inside like a burglar. The lamp in the corner casts a dim light, and there's Evelyn, lying still in bed, wearing the same red floral dress. She hasn't moved since I last saw her. Her face is pale, like a sheet of ice, giving the room a cold, eerie feeling. There's no way she could've been standing at the top of the stairs.

I'm getting more paranoid by the minute. Dr. Whitman would have something to say about this, but I refuse to let my thoughts go that far.

Jack's sudden voice startles me.

"What are you doing here?" he says.

I jump up and yelp. Jack is standing behind me; I feel his unwavering presence.

"I'm...I'm just checking up on Evelyn." I look at her lifeless body, then back at Jack, giving him a small smile.

"I see," Jack says. "You're so nosy, Emily. I've told you I would take care of this, haven't I?"

"Of course, Jack." My voice oozes sweetness. "I came to check up on her. I thought I saw her standing at the top of the stairs earlier."

Jack scoffs. "Oh, Emily. Don't be silly. I called a doctor today. He said Evelyn would be fine, and she shouldn't be bothered. She just needs to rest."

"You did?" Surprise washes over me. "What's wrong with her? Did the doctor say?"

"She just had a concussion, that's all. But she will be fine," he says coldly.

"Oh." I'm genuinely relieved to hear him say this. "What's the timeline?"

"Timeline?" Jack says. "It's hard to tell. He said if she wasn't fully recovered by the end of the week to call back."

"End of the week? That's like, tomorrow."

"That's right," Jack says in a mocking voice, as if I'm an imbecile. "Let's go to bed now."

He comes behind me and puts his hand on the small of my back, pushing me forward. We ascend the stairs to the bedroom, Jack whispering something.

I turn around and ask, "What did you say?"

He snaps his head and creases his forehead. "What? I didn't say anything."

We come to the landing where I stand, looking at Jack,

chuckling nervously. "Come on, Jack. You said something. I heard you whispering."

"Emily." His annoyance is palpable. "Cut the shit, will you? I didn't say anything."

He walks by me and enters the bedroom, me shuffling behind him. "Are you messing with me right now, Jack?"

He's taking off his clothes, ready to dive into bed, "Emily, are you hearing voices again?"

Or am I getting too paranoid?

I place my hands on my hips. "What do you mean 'again?' Are you remembering that one time I heard voices, and it ended up being a cat outside? Totally can't even compare."

"Just drop it, Emily. I didn't say a word. Let's just go to bed, since I'm tired and need to be up early. Peter is arriving early again."

Oh, yes. Peter and his crew. Speaking of which...there's something else that's been bothering me. There's so much mystery around here that I can't keep track of what's real and what isn't.

"Jack, have you noticed some of our food missing in the kitchen?"

Jack turns sharply toward me. "Like what?"

"We had a whole box of crackers in the cabinet and the entire block of Munster cheese is gone. You don't think...?"

"Are you saying Peter or his men snooped around the kitchen and ate our food?" Jack snaps.

I slide into our bed, feeling uneasy. Why would complete strangers help themselves to our food? That doesn't sit well with me. It feels violating. I would never do it to somebody else without getting their permission first.

"Yeah, that's what I'm saying."

Jack immediately dismisses me, like my concern shouldn't matter. "So what? It's just a box of crackers and cheese. Since when did you get so stingy?"

"I'm not..." before I come to my defense, I stop, as our argument will only spiral out of control. "Never mind. Good night, Jack."

He leans forward and kisses me on the lips. A quick one. "Good night, Emily. Let's take it easy, okay? I'm confident Evelyn will get better soon and go home."

I smile and nod. "Okay."

Jack falls asleep almost immediately. But my thoughts are running wild, preventing me from falling asleep. Gosh, I wish I didn't worry so much, filling myself with such constant anxiety.

Could Peter really have eaten our food? Why not? Maybe one of them got peckish and rummaged around in the kitchen until they found something easy to kill their hunger.

Of course, they could have, unless...

I sit up in bed suddenly, my heart racing. What if it

wasn't Peter? What if it wasn't anyone on his team? My mind drifts back to Evelyn—standing at the top of the stairs, or at least I thought I saw her there. But that's impossible, isn't it? She's been unconscious for days, right?

I glance at Jack, his steady breathing suggesting he's in a deep sleep. The house is so quiet, but I can't shake the feeling that something is off. Maybe I'm just tired, or maybe it's the alcohol still messing with my mind. But the more I think about it, the more the pieces don't seem to fit.

I hear a creak from downstairs.

I freeze, my pulse quickening. Was that the house settling? Or...someone moving around? My stomach twists in knots as I listen intently, straining to hear any other sound.

Nothing.

I exhale heavily and lie back down, pulling the covers tightly around me.

Maybe tomorrow will bring clarity, or maybe things will get worse.

But I can't help but wonder... how long can I keep pretending everything is fine?

CHAPTER 26

Emily

IN THE MORNING, I find a strange envelope sitting on the kitchen island.

I don't remember seeing it there when I'd arrived home last night, which can only mean that the workers found it at the front door and brought it in this morning.

I pick it up hesitantly, as if it's burning, and flip it over. The envelope is addressed to me, the handwriting oddly familiar, though I can't place it. There's no postage or sender's name. It was clearly hand-delivered, but by who?

Peter shows up out of nowhere, holding a tool in his hand. "Good morning."

"Hi," I say, thinking about that box of crackers. Should I ask?

"Did you see the envelope I left over there?"

I nod. "I did. Thank you."

"Oh, good. I found it at the door. You couldn't really miss it." He laughs softly.

"Did you...did you see who delivered it, by any chance?" My voice is shaky, but I do my best to control it.

Peter shakes his head. "Nope. It was there when I arrived."

This gets me even more curious. I need to open it right away and see for myself what's inside.

I put the envelope under my shirt and head for the half-bathroom off the kitchen. With shaky hands, I turn on the lights, lock the door behind me, and sit on the toilet, eagerly anticipating what's inside.

The envelope is barely sealed. I pull the edges and place my hand inside, carefully patting the insides of the envelope with my fingers. At the edge, I feel another piece of thicker paper. I pull it out and see right away that it's a photo.

I gasp.

The photo is a grainy, old Polaroid-style picture taken at night. In the foreground, it shows a younger Jack standing beside a damaged car with a shattered headlight and a cracked windshield. His face is contorted, eyes wide with shock or panic. He's looking down at something—or someone —on the ground just out of the frame, but a part of a leg or arm shows in the photo, suggesting a person lying injured or worse.

The background includes a desolate, dimly lit road, maybe near some woods or an isolated area, heightening the eerie atmosphere. There's a smear of blood on the car's bumper, adding to the implication of the hit-and-run.

I fight the urge to retch.

"Oh my God," I hear myself whisper, and the dizziness takes over my vision as fear hits me like a heavy brick.

Someone out there wants me to know about Jack's past. But what else do they know?

Do they know that the person lying on the road, supposedly dead, is Grace Holloway?

The victim of Jack's hit-and-run?

I glance back at the door, listening for any sound from the house. Peter is still out there working, and Jack will be down soon enough, but I can't let them see this. Not yet. I need to process what I'm seeing and what it means.

But as I sit there, the weight of the situation settles deeper. This is no ordinary photo, no casual reminder of the past. It's a threat. Someone knows what Jack did. Someone wants me to know, too.

I fear someone might have discovered my reason for marrying Jack.

I shove the photo back into the envelope, my fingers shaking uncontrollably. I put it in the vanity below the sink, tucking it in between the toilet supplies. It's well hidden there, and it's a place Jack would never consider looking.

I stand up on unsteady legs and splash some cold water on my face. The droplets on my skin feel refreshing. I look at myself in the mirror and see a troubled gaze. I don't remember the last time I've been concerned about my safety. Dr. Whitman might be right—I am playing with fire instead of just coming out clean, squaring it with Jack, telling him I know all about the hit-and-run.

And that he got away with it.

Jack will never be able to trust me again. But what's worse: leaving someone on the road for the dead, or pretending to marry for love? Both Jack and I have kept our secret from each other, one heavier than the other.

Does his mother know about the hit-and-run? And something else: she's here to patch things up and to remind Jack she is the reliable mother who keeps him out of trouble. It makes me wonder what else Jack has done to keep out of jail. What else is Jack capable of doing and getting away with?

I do my best to gather my thoughts. One thing is certain —I can't confront Jack about this. My plan for revenge could be ruined.

My heart thumps as I square my face in the mirror, working on removing all traces of agitation before Jack sees it. I take deep, cleansing breaths and steady my shaking hands. No one can find out about the photo, especially not Jack. That can of worms needs to remain closed.

I unlock the bathroom door, step back into the kitchen, and force myself to smile as Peter walks by with a hammer in his hand. Everything in me screams to keep calm, to act normal. But inside, my world has just been turned upside down.

For now, I'll have to pretend that everything is fine.

Whoever sent that envelope—they must be watching.

CHAPTER 27

THE MEMORY of Jack from our first meeting is still vivid in my mind.

It was a stormy night in Boston, when the northeaster blew in more snow than expected. My friends and I found ourselves stuck at the W Hotel downtown, sipping drinks by the bar. But I hadn't chosen that spot at random. I knew Jack would be there—his friend had tagged him on social media, confirming their plans for the night.

On my way to the hotel, my heart raced. I wasn't sure what I expected, but the pull was undeniable. This would be the first time I'd met Jack—the man who'd left a person for dead on a Seattle road many moons ago. A shiver ran through me at the thought of facing a killer, the person responsible for relentless anxiety and fractured memory. But my resolve to get close to him, to undo what he'd done, was stronger than my fear. He needed to pay.

While the storm outside raged, the hotel lobby was warm, buzzing with the clink of glasses and muted conversations. And then I saw him. Jack was sitting with his back to me, laughing with his friends, completely unaware of my presence.

I settled in, ordering a stiff drink while keeping my eyes on Jack. His movements were smooth, exuding confidence. His tall, handsome stature was intimidating. He could easily be mistaken for someone who poses for a men's magazine. That day, I'd worn my black dress, which revealed just enough cleavage, and I applied extra makeup. I wanted to measure up to Jenna, the stunning beauty, who'd questioned why I looked so different.

But I couldn't tell her.

The wintery mix blowing by the windows seemed quite charming at first; the views breathtaking, with the snow covering the streets of Boston and making everything white.

As the evening progressed, the snow grew taller, slowing the traffic down and turning the night into a hazard.

Having drinks brightened up the mood.

We were yapping about old times, sipping our martinis and catching up on everything we'd missed over the last couple of years. It was refreshing to see both Marcia and Jenna, though I felt distracted. It was hard to fully switch off, thanks to all the stress that had piled up at work. Still, I pushed those thoughts aside and let myself relax, diving into the conversation and enjoying the comfort of our reunion.

As the snow piled up and the wind howled louder, it became clear that we wouldn't be going anywhere for the night.

It wasn't until much later, when the crowd braved the storm and the bar began to thin and quiet down, that Jack first laid eyes on me. He was sitting a few stools away, casually sipping a scotch. His dark hair was slightly messy, his jawline sharp under the low light, and there was something about the way he looked—calm and confident, like nothing could ever really bother him.

Our eyes met for a brief moment, and there he was, standing up and walking toward me with a casual ease, as though we'd known each other for years.

"Snow's really coming down out there," he said with a small smile, and I could hear the warmth in his voice.

I smiled back, despite myself. "Yeah, looks like we're snowed in."

"Oh shoot," he threw his head back, "I forgot to lock my igloo."

We both laughed at his quip.

"Hey, would you like another drink?" I asked. I couldn't believe I'd finally come across Jack. I tried to push away the nerves and the giddiness. I couldn't, in a million years, mess this up.

Jack fidgeted and ran his fingers over his hair. "You know." He looked at me, embarrassed. "I really shouldn't."

My eyes bulged at him. "You've already had too much? I get it, snow will do it to you."

He chuckled with borderline cuteness. "I wish that was the reason."

I sipped what little was left in my glass and watched him over the rim, studying his facial expression. Guilt. Remorse. Even pride? I knew the real reason, but I challenged him. "So, what is it, then, if you don't mind me asking?"

He looked at his glass and swirled it over and over, the last ice cube melting into the water. "Well, let's just say I messed up a long time ago." He drank the last sip, then put his glass down on the bar.

I didn't want to challenge him further, fearing I'd drive him away. "Oh, let's leave it at that, then."

After all, I already knew all the details.

Jack had been caught the night of the hit-and-run, close to his house. At first, the accident was tied to him, but in the end, all he was charged with was a DUI. His lawyer managed to get the more serious charges dropped. He lost his driver's license for a year and had to do a month of community service—that was it. His lawyer argued there was no clear evidence that the accident was tied to her client.

But I knew better.

In simple words, a young woman's life had been weighed against the future of a rising star in the law sector, and he'd come out on top. Rich, white men have it so easy.

"You should have a drink if you want to," Jack said.

"It's okay. I've had enough myself."

I glanced at Jenna, whose eyes were shooting daggers at me from across the room. I knew she was interested in Jack, but she couldn't have him.

He was mine now, and I wasn't letting him go.

CHAPTER 28

Emily

WHEN I ARRIVE AT WORK, Claire senses a different vibe from me. "Oh my. Is everything okay?"

Her concern for me is undeniable. She sits across from my desk and leans forward, waiting to hear all about it. I can't tell her about the photo of Jack. No one can find out. Not yet. But she already knows about my troubles with Evelyn, so I might as well tell her about her unfortunate fall and how she ended up in a coma...or whatever it is.

"That's terrible," Claire whispers. "It sounds like a scene from a horror movie. What are you going to do?"

"Jack told me he's taking care of it." But now that I've seen the photo, it makes me wonder. Could Jack have been lying this whole time?

"I guess he's taking care of his mother," Claire continues, as if to make sense of what I'm saying. "When my mother came for a visit from Iowa, she had some health issues, and we ended up calling her doctor back home to transfer her medical records. Did Jack do the same?"

I slowly shake my head. "No. Actually, I'm not sure."

"Well, if you're not sure, I highly suggest you call her doctor back in...was it Seattle?"

"Yeah."

"You'll know if she's had a history of similar episodes, or whatever."

"Right." Claire makes sense. She always does.

"And if I'm being honest with you, the whole situation seems very weird."

I flinch in my seat. Everything is weird, I agree, but I ask Claire, "Which part?"

"The fact that she's been unconscious for this long. I've never heard of such a thing, not without someone needing to be in hospital under constant observation." She shrugs her shoulders. "But what the hell do I know? I'm not a health expert." She laughs to ease my concern. "I have to be honest with you, though. If I were you, I would send her to the hospital right away. Like, immediately."

That evening, when I come home, as I watch Evelyn, a wave of clarity hits me. I had told myself Jack was right, that she would be fine on her own—unconscious or not. But now,

I realize I've been fooling myself. The truth I hadn't wanted to face is glaringly obvious: Evelyn needs medical help, and I've been too shaken, too overwhelmed, to see it. I can't ignore this any longer. 'She has to go to the hospital,' I say, my voice firmer than I expected.

I get online to look for the phone number for the Seattle hospitals. When Jack told me about Evelyn's heart surgery, if it did happen, he said it was done at St. Francis hospital. That much I remember.

I locate the main number and dial. I'm aware that the doctors can't help me unless I provide them with Evelyn's personal information, but what am I going to lose? The sad part is that I still know little about my mother-in-law. I don't know what year she was born, where she was born, or how many, if any, siblings she has. The only thing that I've learned is that she used to be a lawyer and likes to crash at people's houses uninvited.

A dispatcher on the other line answers, "St. Francis Hospital, how may I help you?"

"Hi." My voice is barely a whisper, as I'm afraid someone might overhear me, even though there's zero chance of that. I'm in our bedroom bathroom with both doors closed. It's only five p.m., and Jack is still working. And Evelyn—well, she's supposedly in a coma. Peter and his crew are nearly done—in a record time, God bless them—and already left the house for the day. Between the half-dead lady in the guest room and the mysterious mail at our door, I bet Peter can't wait to get the hell out of dodge and never return.

"Hi," I repeat. "I'm calling to request my medical records, please." I clear my throat. "I'm in Boston for a visit, but I haven't been feeling well lately, and I wanted to get my medical records before I go see a doctor."

There's silence on the other end. "What's your name?"

A sliver of encouragement sparks inside. "My name is Evelyn Ross. I had a heart surgery at your hospital recently."

I'm not really sure if I'm going to pull this off. But if I pretend I'm Evelyn, my chances of getting her medical records may increase.

There's a pause. "A heart surgery? Can you hold on for a second?"

"Sure."

The dispatcher puts me on hold, and music comes on. Classical music. It's supposedly on to help pass the time more quickly, but it's just getting on my nerves. I roll my eyes —why not pick something more contemporary that most of us are familiar with?

My thoughts get disrupted when another voice on the other line greets me. "Hello? Is this... Mrs. Ross?" He sounds hesitant, almost confused.

"It is."

"Hi. I'm Doctor Jackson. May I ask what you're looking for?"

"Yes, sure, Doctor Jackson. I've been visiting my son in Boston and have not been feeling well. I'd love to go see a doctor here, but was told I needed my medical records. Is it possible to have those?"

I know the odds are low.

"I'm sorry, but there has to be some confusion here."

"What...what do you mean?"

"Mrs. Evelyn Ross had her heart surgery two weeks ago and is still at the hospital recovering. Could there be a different Evelyn Ross we're talking about?"

I feel the room tilt slightly, my grip tightening around the phone. "Excuse me, Doctor Jackson, can you repeat that?"

"You can't be Mrs. Evelyn Ross, because Mrs. Ross is still recovering here at St. Francis," he says calmly, as though what he's saying is completely normal. But nothing about this is normal.

I swallow hard, my mind racing. "That can't be right," I stammer, trying to process the information. "I've been staying here in Boston for the past week. I... was in a coma. I fell down yesterday." I'm falling apart; my words trail off slowly.

There's a pause on the other end. "I'm sorry, but the Mrs. Evelyn Ross who had surgery here is still under our care," Doctor Jackson says, his voice laced with concern. "Perhaps this is some kind of misunderstanding?"

My heart is pounding in my chest, my mind spinning

with confusion and disbelief. I grip the phone harder, trying to keep my voice steady. "There's no misunderstanding," I whisper. "I am Evelyn. I'm sure of it." But my voice comes out hollow, stripped of confidence.

I've dug a bit of a hole here.

Another silence fills the line before Doctor Jackson speaks again. "I'm sorry, whoever you are. The Evelyn Ross I'm referring to was admitted weeks ago and hasn't been discharged. I recommend you reach out to her family members to clarify."

Family members? What family members? Jack—is he even a family member?

He continues, "She has mentioned her son Jack a few times. Do you know him?"

Oh, my God.

I can barely speak, but I manage a faint "thank you" before ending the call. My hand trembles as I set the phone down on the counter, my thoughts spiraling out of control.

If Evelyn is still in Seattle recovering from heart surgery...then who is the woman currently lying in a coma in my home?

I sit on the edge of the bathtub, the cold tiles pressing into my legs as the gravity of the situation hits me. My breath comes in shallow gasps as I try to make sense of it all. This doesn't make any sense. How could Evelyn be in two places at once?

Except she isn't. A terrifying thought. The woman in my home isn't Evelyn at all. She's someone else, someone who's been pretending to be Jack's mother all along. And so has Jack.

A sense of extreme anxiety envelopes me. I'm hardly able to breathe. Seconds later, I plunge onto the floor, and deep darkness takes over.

CHAPTER 29

Jack

I COME HOME AROUND EIGHT, and Emily is not in the living room or the kitchen. We have an open concept house, so it's not like I'd miss her when I first enter.

"Hello!" I call out an Emily-like greeting, but to no response. Where is she?

I leave my briefcase on the couch and go to the kitchen, opening the fridge to get a beer. It's been a rough day, but thank God it's Friday. Between the demanding client and using all my brainpower to outsmart Evelyn, I'm simply worn out.

I lie down on the couch, spreading my arms and legs, a beer bottle in my hand. Unsure of my next move, I just stare at the ceiling.

Well, for now, I should text Emily and see if she's coming home soon. I pull out my phone.

Hey, babe, where are you? You having
dinner with Jenna again? :)

It's supposed to be a cute, non-accusatory text, though I would be remiss if I didn't admit it would be strange for her to see Jenna again tonight.

I've never told Emily what a snake her friend Jenna is. After Emily and I started dating, Jenna stole my number from Emily's phone and texted me, spilling all the worst things about her, then asked me out. Sure, Jenna's a knock-out, no doubt about that. But if she can do this to one of her so-called best friends, she's not the person I'd want by my side for life.

Besides, I've done so much hard work to upend my life and erase my past, so the last thing I would do is add unfaith-fulness to my list of transgressions.

I haven't told Emily about Jenna, because I didn't want her to worry. I don't want her to lose a friendship over a minor hurdle that happened in the past and nothing ever materialized. It's enough for one of us to know what kind of person Jenna is.

After thirty minutes, Emily still doesn't respond.

"Ha," I say to myself. "I guess I should go to bed."

On my way there, I walk past the guest room and check

up on Evelyn. Sure enough, she's still resting in her same position. I'm not even sure how she can keep up this vegetative state for so long. It's quite possible she's pretending, like the first time, and it's possible she sneaks in the kitchen and eats our food to sustain herself. And honestly, that's fine with me.

In the meantime, I had set up the IV drip by Evelyn's bedside, carefully taping the tubes to her arm. I explained to Emily that the doctors had come by while she was at work and had set this up to keep Evelyn hydrated until she regained consciousness. Emily nodded, relieved, but I sensed a flicker of doubt as her eyes darted over the machines. She wanted to believe me, to believe I had everything under control.

Evelyn will be gone soon either way.

As soon as I finish doing her a favor.

Upstairs, I push open the bathroom door, my heart pounding in my chest. The sight of Emily crumpled on the floor knocks the air out of me. She's lying there, limp, her body splayed awkwardly on the cold tile. Her face is pale, almost ghostly, and her breathing—it's so shallow, so faint—I can barely see her chest rise and fall. My stomach twists into knots as I drop to my knees beside her. "Emily!" My voice cracks, shaking with panic. I reach out, but I'm terrified to touch her, terrified I might hurt her more.

I take Emily's lifeless body into my arms and carry her to

bed. I place her there slowly, moving her disheveled hair to the side and checking on her breathing again. She's alive. But barely. "Fuck."

I'm doing my best not to panic. Unlike for Evelyn, I call the ambulance, afraid she is terribly hurt. I get a hold of an EMT and am told they should be here soon.

After ten minutes, I hear the sirens blowing along the street until they come closer and halt. The two men walk in with a poker face, asking me where my wife is. As we ascend the stairs, I'm praying she will be fine.

The EMTs check her vitals and ask about her medical history.

"Is she prone to falls?" one of the EMTs, a younger guy with cheek dimples, turns to me and asks.

"Falls? Not that I know of."

In reality, I don't know much about Emily's medical history. In the back of my mind, I remember her mention something about once being in a coma, but the details elude me. She didn't want to divulge much more. She said it was so long ago. Emily likes to keep things private. Like her anxiety pills. Besides taking those, she hasn't told me she takes anything else, but can I trust her at this point?

"Any idea what could have caused a fall?"

I slowly shake my head and think. Emily likes to drink, but I've never seen her hammered out of her mind. "I have no idea."

"Is she pregnant, by any chance?"

"Pregnant?" I widen my eyes at the EMT. Could Emily be pregnant and she hasn't told me yet? "No, I don't think she is, sir." But as I say this, I'm unsure of myself.

The EMT looks at me quizzically, as if I could have something to do with her fall. Does he think I pushed her or something? I would never in a million years.

"Sir, you have no clue how your wife might have fallen?" the other EMT says. His voice is accusatory, but I ignore it.

"No. I wasn't here. When I came home from work, I found her lying on the bathroom floor."

They ignore me and check Emily's vitals again.

I'm standing behind them and awaiting their verdict. What is wrong with Emily?

As if reading my mind, the shorter one turns around and tells me it's a severe concussion, most likely from hitting the edge of the bathtub. Emily needs to rest, but she will be fine. If she doesn't wake up in the morning, she should go to the hospital. But I still might take her, because I couldn't bear the thought of something serious happening to Emily. She should stay away from work for a week and from strenuous physical activities.

Rest rest rest.

"Oh, and one more thing." The EMT scratches his face. "She might lose some long-term memory."

"I'm sorry. What? Did you say she might lose some memory?"

"Yes. it's normal with this type of concussion, though it is not permanent. It might restore at some point with healthy diet, hydration, and exercise."

"Oh, Jesus."

"I'm sorry, sir. But be glad it's not worse than it is."

Worse. It's not worse. It's better. It's great.

With Emily losing her long-term memory, I can only hope she will forget all the mishaps that occurred since Evelyn arrived.

I need to think fast about what to do with Evelyn. She's still lying in the bed of our guest room, taking the space, breathing our air. She needs to be gone before Emily wakes up and regains her memory.

How can I get rid of her before things spiral out of control? There's no doubt Emily will find out about Evelyn's true identity, sooner or later. She's already on the path. I will have a lot of explaining to do, and I don't know if I'm ready.

The EMT pulls me out of my stupor and says, "I think we should take her to the ER, just in case."

I nod. "Okay. Okay. Let's do it."

At the ER, the doctor—who seems frantic and busy— approaches me with the results. "Your wife's head CT scan is negative. However, she does have a concussion, as indi- cated by her amnesia. We've observed her and believe it's safe for her to return home, as long as someone can monitor her. She may remain drowsy for a while, as she had an elevated alcohol level. She should rest and avoid work or driving until her memory issues resolve. Okay?"

I nod, feeling immense relief.

After the ER, I take Emily home and settle her into bed immediately. Her eyes are tightly shut, and her face is as pale as a ghost.

I take Emily's phone. I open her phone; I know all her passwords, and I see my text was delivered but not read. I check what numbers she's called recently. The last number she dialed has a Seattle phone number. I push the redial button, and someone at St. Francis Hospital answers the phone.

I push the end call button, realizing Emily must have called to check on Evelyn's medical records. If not that, then I am not sure what other reason she'd call.

I can't help but think Emily is suspecting something. I'm almost positive Emily must know now that the woman lying in our guest room is not her mother-in-law.

She has been acting strange the past day and I can't put my finger on why. I can only surmise she has dug about Evelyn's past, and if she hasn't, it's a matter of time. I've noticed she is uncomfortable with her being in the house, and I should probably do something to get her out.

But Evelyn is a stubborn bitch.

She won't quit until she gets her way.

I sit on the edge of the bed, watching Emily's chest rise and fall, each breath shallow but steady. The EMTs said she'd be fine, that it was just a bad concussion, but their words do little to ease my nerves. Her pale face haunts me, reminding me of how fragile this all is, how close I am to losing control. I brush a strand of hair from her forehead, my hand trembling.

The whole situation has spiraled faster than I ever anticipated.

I know Evelyn won't stop. She's like a dark shadow looming over everything, refusing to leave until she gets what she came for. And now Emily—she's caught in the crossfire of this mess, a mess I created. My mind races, thinking about her phone call to St. Francis, and how close Emily came to uncovering the truth. I can't let that happen.

I need to handle Evelyn, and I need to do it soon. But how? She's manipulative, cunning—she knows too much. Every option feels like a trap, pulling me deeper into something darker. But the longer she stays, the more I risk losing everything. I can't let her destroy my life, my marriage.

Not after everything.

I lean down and press my lips softly to Emily's forehead, whispering, "I'll fix this, my love." My gaze lingers on her fragile, helpless figure. I take a breath and add, "I promise."

But the words sound hollow, even to me.

CHAPTER 30

Jack

"AREN'T YOU LUCKY?" Evelyn sits in the living room chair, arms and legs crossed. She's rocking that hanging leg like her life depends on it. She has been awake ever since she learned Emily has had a concussion.

Evelyn is like a zombie that comes out of her grave and haunts you until she eats you alive. She never quits.

"Lucky? What do you mean?" I retort.

"I heard what the EMT said about Emily's long-term memory. I guess you might get away with all your lies, after all," she laughs.

I scoff, "Stop it."

"Oh, Jack. You look like a frightened turtle." She giggles. "I don't remember you being such a pussy."

"Shut up, you damn fool," I shout, harder than I intended.

She laughs again.

I sit down on the sofa, my legs apart, my hands buried in my face. Think think think. Evelyn has put me in a pickle. I'm so frazzled. But if I don't do what she asks me, I will never be able to get rid of her.

In the end, it's easier just to take the plunge and do it.

"She's got you wrapped up around her finger. Huh, Jack?" Evelyn laughs mockingly. "She has so much control over you that you don't have the balls to do what's right."

That's when I know I've had enough. All my pent-up anger is bursting at the seams.

I bolt out of the chair and go straight for Evelyn's neck. The wineglass in her hand drops on the floor and shatters into pieces. The wine spills on the Persian rug, leaving more stains. I tighten my grip, my fingers digging into her skin, and for a moment, I see pure terror in her bulging eyes. She gasps, trying to claw at my hands, her breath coming out in ragged, desperate gulps. But I can't stop now—the rage inside me is boiling over, blinding me to everything.

On my second attempt to harm Evelyn, I can only hope she will change for the better, learn her lesson. But she's a tough nut to crack—she's like a cockroach that refuses extinction. But God damn it, I've had enough of her.

All I can think of is the turmoil she's brought into our

lives. She came here—uninvited—to ruin everything I've built in life, putting all the terrible memories behind and starting over. How do I get rid of her for good?

She finds her strength and peels my fingers off her. Her violent cough gets me out of my raging stupor, and I take a couple of steps back to compose myself.

She kneels on the floor and keeps coughing to regain her bearings. I almost killed her. Anger inside me finally subdues when I think of the consequences. I imagine disposing of her body; the cops knocking on my door for interrogation.

Just like once before.

I avoided a sentence in the past, but I highly doubt I would this time.

Evelyn sits up and leans against the chair. She's looking at me in surrender, as if she's ready to do whatever is necessary to make things work, to reach a deal.

After she takes a deep exhale, she says, "Okay, Jack. Let's make a proper plan. I'll make it easy on you, I promise."

CHAPTER 31

Emily

Fucking hell. The headache is unbearable.

"Ugh."

I open my eyes slowly, feeling the beat pulsing in my head. I'm in a dark room, the sun peeking between the window curtains, its gentle rays landing on the bed. The air feels stale and heavy. I gasp for it, my breath catching in my throat. Being awake feels nauseating.

When I first woke up in the hospital this morning, a man was sitting at my bedside, watching me with a worried intensity. His face was kind, familiar vaguely that I couldn't place, yet there was an unsettling emptiness where my memory of him should have been. He introduced himself as Jack, my husband, and though the word felt foreign, he held my hand, promising that the memories would return in time.

"I'll take you home," he hissed. "Everything will feel right again soon."

I wanted to believe him, to trust that the warmth in his gaze was a sign of the life we'd shared, even if it eluded me now.

I reach for my head, which is throbbing as if someone beat me all night long. I'm sort of aware of my surroundings, but everything feels hazy, like I'm seeing through a fog. I quickly orient myself: I'm lying in bed, slightly propped on a pillow behind me.

A woman is sitting in a chair beside my bed, reading. She is gripping a book tightly and looks pensive. Her bun on top of her head looks strikingly messy. She has too much makeup on her face, as if she's trying to conceal something.

Who is she?

I don't remember seeing her before. Why is she here, in my house? Is this my house at all? My eyes dart around the room as I try to make sense of the place.

It looks familiar...but something feels off. The bedsheet is a color I should know, but it feels strangely distant (I'd never choose pink), as if I'm seeing it through someone else's eyes. My gaze shifts across the room to a framed photograph on the wall, and I squint to make it out. Two people—me, I realize, and a man—are smiling at each other.

We look happy, though there's a shadow of sadness in my eyes. My brown hair swept to one side, just like I wear it now.

The man beside me must be my husband. We're at the beach, but I can't remember that day at all.

As I make a slight movement, the woman by my side lifts her head from the book. She leans forward and plasters a wide, creepy smile onto her face. Her big white teeth don't seem real. I rub my eyes to better assess her.

I still don't recognize her.

"Hi, dear. You're awake," she whispers.

"Hi." My voice is raspy. I need water.

"Can I get you something to drink? Water?"

I nod ever so slightly. Any movement causes the headache to amplify. I don't remember what caused it, or why I'm lying in bed with my body feeling like a train wreck. I don't remember anything, and that scares me. The woman next to me seems to be here to care for me, even though I don't know who she is and whence she came.

She carefully places her book facedown on the nightstand, then takes the cane resting beside it. Rising slowly from her chair, she leans on the cane as she heads toward the door. She doesn't look quite old enough to need it, so I wonder if she might have been injured.

Her walk is wobbly, her movements erratic. Sometimes, we can recognize people by their subtle movements, but watching this woman walk across the bedroom still doesn't ring any bells.

I look around to search for evidence of what prompted me to be bedbound and I search my memory, but there's absolutely nothing.

The strange woman walks through the door, holding a glass of water. She approaches my side of the bed and puts the water glass on the nightstand next to her book. "Let me help you up."

She nuzzles me off the pillow and places another one behind me, so I can sit up. "Here. Let me get you water."

I eagerly sip the water, quenching the thirst accumulated over God knows how long. The liquid seems to do wonders, and it invigorates me instantly. "How long have I been asleep? What happened to me?"

She cocks her head and puts that creepy smile on again. "Oh. You just had a little fall in the bathroom. The doctor says it's a concussion, but you should heal soon."

I sigh. "Gosh, I guess it makes sense. I don't remember anything." I scan the woman's face, her creepy smile still lingering. "What day is it, anyway?"

"Saturday." It's all she says.

She tilts her head, left and right, studying me with that fixed smile, as if it's glued onto her lips.

"What's your name?"

"My name?" She points a finger at herself. "I'm Misty."

"Misty?" I sip water. I don't remember any Mistys.

She leans against the chair and crosses her legs. "I'll be taking care of you, love."

She smiles at me again, then picks up the book from the nightstand, gives me a quick glance, and starts reading.

She's making me feel uncomfortable, and surely, I'm supposed to be comfortable in my own home.

"Misty. If I may." I clear my throat and pull the sheets a little tighter.

Misty looks at me, her brows furrowed, as if annoyed I'm disrupting her reading. "What?"

"What else did the doctor say? Can I go back to work soon?"

I don't remember what exactly it is that I do, but I'm sure it will all come back to me. I just know that I have a job that keeps me busy.

Misty huffs and puts the book on her lap, gesturing more annoyance. "Don't you think you should be resting and recovering and not worrying about work?"

I nod. "I guess."

"Well, if you really want to know, the doctor said you shouldn't be working for at least a week until you're fully recovered.

"A week?" I don't remember the last time I took that many sick days. But then again, not that I remember much of anything right now. And it's driving me crazy.

"That's right, love. I'll be taking care of you until you recover. And to recover, you need to stay in bed and rest up." She's looking down on me like I'm in trouble. "Can I get you anything else? Are you hungry?"

I shake my head slowly. "No. I don't feel any hunger right now." I pull the sheet closer and ball it in my fist. The woman's presence, her scolding voice, doesn't comfort me like it should. I can only assume Jack hired her to be around while he's at work. Even if I don't remember much at the moment, I can only assume Jack means well and wants me to be taken care of.

That afternoon, Misty stays by my side, occasionally running to the kitchen to get me water and food and meds for my headache. I can't say I've been hungry, but she insists I eat so I can feel better soon.

I have so many questions, but my mind is clouded, and I can't think straight.

"Misty, can you please help me up? I need to use the bathroom."

"Oh. Sure." She stands up immediately and takes my arm, pulling me like I'm a rope in a tug of war.

My legs are wobbly, but I manage to walk across the bedroom floor and get to the bathroom. Misty is by my side, holding onto my arm so tight as if she is afraid I'll escape. Even if I tried, I don't have enough strength.

When we get to the bathroom, Misty looks at me. "Do you want me to stay, or are you good?"

I grab the edge of the sink for support. "I'm good." I give her a small smile to reassure her before she changes her mind.

Misty turns around and sits back in the chair, looking at the bathroom. She slowly disappears from my view as I close the door. "Don't lock the door!" Her muffled voice travels through the air.

"Okay," I yell out.

In an attempt to regain my memory, I look around the bathroom to seek clues. But the walls and the tiles and the tub are all nondescript and don't reveal anything about my life.

I open the medicine cabinet, hoping to see small clues about my life tucked inside, but as my eyes scan the shelves, all I see is a can of shaving cream, a cologne, and a bottle of aspirin.

Useless.

I close the cabinet door and flush the toilet, hoping to make Misty believe I'm actually doing something in there. When I return to the bed, she's staring at me, her eyes filled with unspoken questions. But she shouldn't worry. After all my snooping, I'm just as confused as ever.

CHAPTER 32

Emily

MY HEAD IS STILL murky when I wake up the following day. The headache has somewhat subsided, but it's still very much there. However, Jack is not. He's already gone for the day, leaving the bed empty by my side.

I still can't remember some details of my life, and it's driving me bonkers. My memory is patchy at best. My mind feels like a puzzle with too many missing pieces, and I can't seem to find where they fit. Some things come back to me in flashes—like the way Jack's touch feels warm and comforting, how the house smells like fresh coffee in the mornings, and the way my phone's screen glows when I pick it up, almost instinctively. But then there are the gaps. I don't remember why I married Jack, or why I trusted him enough to let him guide me through this confusing haze. And Misty. Her face looks familiar, but the name? I can't spot her in my mind for the life of me. I know there's something important there, something I should remember, but it slips through my fingers every time I try. I want to make sense of it all, but the more I try, the more everything blurs into confusion.

A slight cough draws my attention. I am not alone.

Misty is sitting in the same chair as yesterday and staring at me. Her expression feels frightening, sending an uneasy feeling down my spine. I draw the sheets closer to my chin, widening my eyes.

As if she senses I am nervous, she plasters on that same creepy smile. "Hi. How are you this morning?"

Her big white teeth look so unnatural in her small head.

I nod, but the movement makes my head feel heavier and uncomfortable. "Better," I muster.

"Are you ready for breakfast?"

"I guess I should eat."

"Okay. Breakfast coming soon."

She trots out of the room with that same unstable walk as yesterday. Now that I think of it, I wonder if she's fit enough to care for me.

While she's preparing breakfast for me, I look for my phone, hoping it will help me reorient myself. Old text messages or phone calls would surely bring some of my memory back, or at least hints of it.

I peek at the nightstand, where I usually keep my phone while sleeping, and don't see it there. I run my hand under the pillow, and it's not there. With some difficulty, I prop myself up and lean forward, opening the nightstand drawer.

My phone isn't there, either.

It's unusual for my phone to disappear, but it's possible I left it somewhere and don't remember.

Just as I'm about to stand up and look around the house, Misty walks through the door. When she sees me standing next to the bed, she widens her eyes and screams, "What do you think you're doing?"

She rushes over to me, leaving a tray of food balanced precariously on the edge of the dresser. Her hands reach for me, and I instinctively shrink back. "You shouldn't be up!" she scolds, her voice sharp. She pushes me all the way to the bed until I lose my balance and plop down.

"I'm just looking for my phone," I say, trying to keep my voice steady, despite the pounding in my head. "I can't seem to remember where I put it."

Misty's face softens, but her eyes dart quickly around the room. "Don't worry about that right now, dear," she says with a forced calmness. "You need to focus on getting better. Everything else can wait."

She pushes me gently back towards the pillow behind, and I relent, too tired and disoriented to argue. But something feels wrong. Why wouldn't she let me look for my phone? And why is she still here? I barely know her.

As I sit down, Misty retrieves the tray she'd abandoned and places it carefully on my lap. "Here," she says, smoothing the surrounding sheets. "Eat up."

I glance down at the food—a simple breakfast of toast, eggs, and fruit—but I'm not hungry. My stomach churns, not from the concussion, but from a growing sense of unease.

Something is off.

"I appreciate your help, but...where's Jack?" I ask, trying to sound casual. "He's usually the one taking care of me when I'm sick."

Misty's smile falters for a fraction of a second before she quickly recovers. "Oh, Jack's very busy with work," she says smoothly. "He asked me to stay and make sure you're alright. You know how dedicated he is."

"But today is Sunday, isn't it? Jack doesn't work on Sundays."

She just sits there and offers a smile.

Something about her doesn't add up, and I need to figure out what's going on before it's too late.

CHAPTER 33

Emily

THE ENTIRE DAY PASSES, and all I do is take naps. There's no question my body needs them.

In between my naps, Jack is nowhere to be found, while Misty is in and out of the room, occasionally hovering over me to see if I need anything. I've already told her I wanted my phone, but she barely acknowledges my pleas. Instead, she repeats I need to rest and get better.

In the afternoon, she picks up the same book she was reading yesterday, and I watch her face grimace into different emotions as she reads. Her reactions to the book are unsettling—too exaggerated for whatever it is she's reading. At one point, she lets out a high-pitched giggle that sends a shiver down my spine. I try not to stare, but it's impossible to look away. I wonder what kind of story could evoke such strange responses?

I glance at the window, hoping to see some sign of the outside world, something to ground me. But all I can see are the blinds, shut tight like they've been since yesterday. The room feels like a cage, and Misty...well, she feels like the warden. It's one thing to help me when I need something, but sitting by my bedside all day? That makes no sense. I'm not so incapacitated that I can't get up and make my own meals. Yet Misty insists on staying.

"So...what are you reading?"

Misty pauses, slowly turning the book over as though she's forgotten the title. "It's called *Do Unto Others* by Mark Jenkins."

I nod, trying to keep it casual. "Oh. Cool. What's it about?"

Her gaze lingers on me for a second too long. She narrows her eyes, the corners of her mouth twitching into a half-smile. "It's about... people paying their dues." Her voice is soft, with an edge that sends a shiver down my spine.

"Where's Jack right now?" I ask, my voice weak but insistent.

Misty briefly gazes at me. "No idea. Not my turn to watch him." She laughs.

I pout and let out a sigh. It's disappointing to hear my husband hasn't been checking in with me and left me with the woman I know nothing about. I should feel grateful that Misty is spending all this time with me, but my frustration about my memory loss mounts. I remember more about Jack than about myself, yet I still don't know enough.

I turn to Misty and ask, "How do you know my husband?"

Misty flips the book on her lap and looks at me. "Your husband?" She fidgets in her seat and clears her throat. "I've known your husband for many years. We're good friends."

She un-flips the book and keeps reading. But her eyes don't seem focused on it; rather, they seem to dance around the page as if in panic.

We're good friends.

This should be common knowledge. Someone I've surely met before or at least heard Jack mention. But again, nothing. It doesn't ring a bell at all. My mind feels like a locked room, and no matter how hard I try, I can't find the key to open it. Misty—her name, her face—none of it stirs even the faintest memory. A total blank.

I search through fragments of conversations with Jack in my mind, trying to recall any mention of her. Still nothing. How could I forget someone important enough to be here now, hovering over me constantly like an annoying mosquito? If she's a friend of Jack's, I would remember. Wouldn't I?

"Are you two...very close?"

She cocks her head, gazes at something beyond me, and nods. "You can say that, yeah." She places her head down, pretending to read.

"Do you know when he will be home?"

She exhales heavily. "I really don't know. Why don't you rest up a little before he comes? Maybe we can have dinner together."

"That sounds good." I smile at Misty, though it feels fake. I need to do anything to convince her I can start taking care of myself. I swing my legs to the side and sit up. "You know what, Misty? I could really use a little walk around the house. Just to stretch my legs. I have been lying in bed for way too long."

She scoffs and stares at me as if considering my request. After several long seconds, she says, "All right. Go ahead. I guess there's no harm in walking around your own house." She lets out a chuckle and goes back to reading her book.

I ease out of bed and quietly make my way to the door, feeling Misty's gaze burning into my back. I slip out, closing the bedroom door softly behind me, and trudge toward the railing, which seems to stretch on endlessly. Looking down the staircase, I flinch. It's much steeper than I remember.

I hold on to the railing, afraid I might fall. Lying in bed for a long period is a sure way to lose muscle strength. As I go down the stairs, the creaking breaks the silence in the house. On the second floor, at the landing, I notice another bedroom, and remember that it's a guest room. Is Misty staying there?

The walk feels like an exploration of a dream I once had. I've seen it all before, and I know it's my home, but the memories of it are hazy.

I keep going until I arrive at the bottom floor. There's a kitchen on my right side, and a living room on my left. I sniff a few times and smell fresh paint, as if someone has just repainted all the walls. Everything looks new and fancy. The house is beautiful, like something you'd find in a glossy spread of Home & Garden magazine.

I stand in the open space between the living room and the kitchen, staring at the walls, trying to make sense of it all. This is supposed to be my house, but it feels so foreign to me, like I've stepped into someone else's life. The furniture, the art on the walls, even the way the light filters through the windows—it's all familiar, yet distant.

The kitchen...I should know this place intimately. I should know how the countertops feel under my fingers, how the floor creaks in certain spots. But as I stand here, nothing triggers a memory. I don't remember what it's like to cook here, to sit at the table with Jack, or even what meals we might have shared. It's as if the details of my life have been erased, leaving only the shell of a home behind.

I walk into the living room, my eyes tracing the lines of the furniture. The couch, dark and sleek, should bring comfort, but it doesn't. It feels too staged, like I'm walking through a showroom. And the photos on the wall—pictures of Jack and me, smiling, laughing—are supposed to be proof of a life lived here, a life shared. But all I see are strangers.

Everything in this house seems meticulously placed, like Jack's been keeping it all together while I... while I what? Forgot? Lost my grip on reality? I can't even remember what I was doing before everything became so hazy. Misty and Jack say I had an accident in the bathroom, but are they telling me the truth?

Outside, a muffled sound of car sirens travels to my ear. Relief washes over me at the reminder that I'm so close to civilization, and not alone in some remote cabin with a person I've never met. Things could be worse.

As I further explore the house, my memories sit on the edge of my conscious, and I keep looking for ways to bring them back, so I can get back to my old self.

There is nothing worse than losing myself.

I walk around the kitchen and look in every corner. Other than another framed photo of Jack and me, there's nothing else that can tie me to my past.

Feeling fatigued suddenly, I hold on to the edge of the kitchen island, my eyes resting on a spot in the living room.

That's when I see it—a glint of something metallic peeking out from under the couch. My heart skips a beat. It could be my phone.

Slowly, I make my way over, careful not to make any noise. I glance over my shoulder, half expecting Misty to appear out of nowhere, her eerie smile plastered on her face. But the house is still and quiet, save for the distant sounds from outside.

When I reach the couch, I kneel and take a better look. There it is—a phone, hidden under the couch, tucked away as if someone didn't want me to find it. My pulse quickens as I snatch it up and study it, reassured this phone belongs to me.

But as soon as I press the power button, my relief fades. The screen is black. Dead. My phone is completely out of battery.

Damn it.

I need a charger, but I can't remember where I'd normally keep one. My eyes dart around the room, searching for a plug or any sign of a charging cable. There's nothing immediately visible. I have to move quickly—Misty could return at any moment, and if she finds me like this, she'll know I've found my phone.

I shove the phone into my pocket and turn back toward the stairs, my mind racing. Maybe there's a charger in the bedroom. If I can just get it charged, maybe I can call Jack or even look at old messages—anything to get some clarity.

As I head back toward the stairs, I hear the soft sound of footsteps. Panic rises in my chest. I freeze, listening carefully.

It's Misty. I hear her coming down the hall, calling my name, her feet padding against the hardwood floor. She's almost at the bottom of the stairs.

Without thinking, I dart into the nearest room—a half bathroom off the kitchen—and press myself against the wall, holding my breath. The footsteps grow louder, and I hear her descending the last of the stairs. My heart is pounding so hard I'm sure she can hear it from the kitchen.

I peek through the crack in the door, just enough to see her. She's standing in the living room now, her eyes sweeping across the space. For a moment, I fear she's going to check the couch, but she doesn't. Instead, she walks over to the photo of Jack and me, her fingers grazing the frame. Her expression hardens, her eyes narrowing slightly, and then she sets the photo back down with deliberate care.

I stay perfectly still, praying she doesn't come any closer.

After what feels like an eternity, she turns and walks back up the stairs. The moment I hear her bedroom door close, I finally exhale, my body trembling with fear and adrenaline.

I need to get my phone charged and find out what's really going on.

CHAPTER 34

Emily

WHEN I ARRIVE in the bedroom, Misty looks outraged. "Where the hell have you been?"

She's talking to me like a child being reprimanded by a principal. "I'm here. I was just...enjoying the house." I approach the bed and slip under the covers.

"Let me tell you. If Jack finds out you've been out of bed for so long, he won't be happy."

I smile and reassure her, "I'm sure Jack will understand."

She shakes her head and rolls her eyes. "My goodness."

Under the covers, I pull out my phone from the pocket and clutch it in my hands like it's a lifeline. Misty and I sit in silence until Misty springs out of the chair and heads for the door. "I'll be back."

As soon as I hear the footsteps fade, I throw back the covers and scramble out of bed. I need to find a charger quickly—it has to be around here somewhere. The nightstand seems like the most obvious place, so I lean forward, glance behind it, and spot a long white cable tangled in the corner.

"Yes," I whisper to myself, excited for the break.

I plug the charger into my phone and hide it behind the nightstand. It's safely tucked in there, and no one should suspect I have it unless they go out of their way to look for it.

About fifteen minutes later, the bedroom door opens, and my chest tightens when I look up, expecting to see Misty, but instead it's Jack.

"Hey." He trudges to the bed to give me a kiss. "How's my princess doing today?" he says with an edge in his voice.

"I'm much better." It's true. I do feel better, even though my memory is still in tatters.

"Oh, good. Misty told me you took a walk around the house today. Please don't exert yourself until you fully recover. Okay?"

"Okay." Silence. "So, where have you been all day?"

"Oh." Jack looks like the question came unexpectedly. "I had to go to the office today. Something urgent came up."

I'm dying to ask what could be so urgent on a Sunday, but I don't, fearing I might find out that Jack does this often. I don't want him to know I'm still struggling.

Jack sits at the edge of the bed, giving me a long stare until he takes my hand. "It seems you're well enough to eat dinner at a table tonight."

I nod. "Totally. I would love that." Being glued to bed for a couple of days has had me all sorts of antsy, so I am truly looking forward to functioning again like a semi-normal person. "So. Misty."

Jack widens his eyes at me. "Yes?"

"She's been good at taking care of me, but how much longer is she staying here? I'm almost fully recovered."

He caresses my hand and looks me in the eye. But his look is hollow, as if he sees through me. "She'll be gone soon." His voice deepens, his gaze lowers. He stands up and turns around, walking in the opposite direction. "We'll order out Chinese if that's okay."

"Oh yeah. I'm excited."

That evening, I join Misty and Jack for dinner at the dining table. I'm as excited as I would be if we were dining in the fanciest restaurant. The table is set simply, with takeout containers scattered across it.

The room feels tense.

Misty sits on Jack's left side, a little too close for my comfort. Her eyes flick to me with that odd smile plastered across her face, the one that never reaches her eyes. Jack sits at the head of the table, his face buried in his phone, only occasionally looking up to offer me a half-hearted smile.

"So," I begin, attempting to break the silence. "What did everyone do today?"

Awkward doesn't even begin to describe the atmosphere.

Misty snorts softly. "Well, I was busy taking care of you, wasn't I?"

I force a laugh, but I really want to punch her. "Yes, of course. I'm very grateful for that."

Jack doesn't look up from his phone, seemingly engrossed in whatever he's scrolling through. "Mm-hmm," he mumbles.

I glance at Misty, who seems content to shovel food into her mouth, but I catch her eyes darting toward Jack now and then, as if she's waiting for something. The discomfort is palpable, and I feel like an intruder in my home.

"Jack," I say softly, trying to pull him back into the conversation. "Tell us what you did. Don't be all mysterious on us." I chuckle.

He finally puts his phone down and looks at me, but his expression is distant. "Oh, the usual." He picks up his chopsticks and fiddles with his food without taking a bite.

I'm not sure what's usual for a Sunday. I nod and smile, hiding any hint that my memory is still at peril.

Misty pipes up, "Oh, Jack. Always doing stuff. I don't know how you do it." Her voice is sugary sweet, but there's an edge to it I can't quite place.

Jack doesn't respond, and the silence stretches on. I

fidget with my napkin, feeling more uncomfortable by the second.

"So," I say again, trying to sound upbeat, "how's the food?"

Misty grins. "It's good, don't you think, Jack? We used to order from this place all the time, back when we were in law school."

Law school? So that's how Misty and Jack met.

Jack clears his throat and finally takes a bite of his food. "Yeah, I guess. It's good," he mutters, avoiding eye contact with both of us.

I feel a pang of something—jealousy, maybe?—but I push it aside. Misty's presence has been more than unsettling lately, and I can't shake the feeling that there's something deeper going on between her and Jack. But now is not the time to bring it up. I need to stay calm, keep the peace. I'm not sure exactly why, but deep down, I feel it's necessary, even though the reasons elude me at the moment.

As we eat in silence, the tension builds. Misty keeps throwing me looks, as if daring me to speak, while Jack seems oblivious to it all, too wrapped up in his own world.

The sound of chewing fills the void, but the awkwardness lingers like a heavy cloud. All I can think about is how badly I want this dinner to end.

When it does, I rush back to bed. Jack joins me shortly after and tells me he's ready to sleep. He doesn't seem to be in a chatty mood, so we kiss each other goodnight. Jack turns around, falling asleep almost immediately. I'm assured his sleep is deep when he starts to snore softly.

I get out of bed and reach for my phone behind the nightstand, now fully charged. To avoid waking up Jack, I go to the bathroom and sit on the toilet, feeling nervous about what my phone holds inside. I hope it will help me refresh my memory, and life will go back to normal. Whatever normal is.

At the outset, I notice a few missed text messages and calls from a person named Claire. I scan through my brain, but I still don't remember her. Reading her messages might help.

But to open the phone, I need my password, which I don't remember. "Ugh."

When everything seems difficult, it just is. There are no corners to cut here.

I bring my phone close to my face, and by some miracle, it unlocks. A flood of messages... and then the realization: I own a catering company. I am Emily Ross. But who is Claire?

I click on Claire's name and read her texts. There's one from yesterday, around 9 a.m.

You left work early yesterday?

That same evening, Claire sent a follow-up text:

> Now you're getting me all worried, Emily. Why are you not responding? Text me back ASAP or call me. Our clients have some questions I can't answer.

Claire is persistent. She texted me again today, threatening to come to my house if I don't answer. That's when it hits me. Claire is my co-worker.

Feeling a sense of relief wash over me, I text Claire back and assure her I'll be at work tomorrow. I'm starting to remember who I am, and the pieces are slowly falling into place. Watertown. My catering company. It all feels familiar now, like a distant dream resurfacing from the fog.

But even as my memories return, there's still one glaring gap in my mind: Misty. I don't remember her at all. Not her voice, not her face, not her presence in my life before this. It's as if she materialized out of thin air, taking up space in my home and between Jack and me. There's something about her that feels off, something that doesn't belong, but I can't quite grasp what it is.

I lean back against the cold bathroom tiles, my phone resting on my lap. My heartbeat has slowed, the tension from dinner fading slightly. At least I'm remembering who I am. That's a good start. Misty remains a mystery, and I need to tread carefully. She's been in the background, watching, waiting—too close to Jack, too involved in our lives.

I glance at the reflection of myself in the bathroom

mirror. I don't recognize the tired, pale woman staring back. But I remind myself that I'm stronger than this. I'll figure out what's going on, piece by piece.

For now, though, I need to rest. Tomorrow will be another day, another chance to reclaim my life. As I return to bed and slip under the covers next to Jack, I resolve to keep my guard up, especially around Misty. Something tells me I haven't uncovered the full story yet.

And until I do, I need to stay vigilant.

CHAPTER 35

Emily

The following day, Monday, I feel good enough to go to work. But Jack won't have it.

"Emily, absolutely not." He raises his voice. "I won't let you walk out of the house in this condition."

"What condition?" I give him a coy smile, spread my arms, and spin around. "I'm feeling good. Don't you see I'm ready to fly the nest?"

Jack shakes his head in protest. "I can't let you drive, Emily. It's too dangerous for someone with a recent concussion. Not to mention you're putting other people in danger, too." A deep fear projects from Jack's eyes.

"I can Uber to the office, don't worry. Plus, I could really use some fresh air and get out of the house. I'm sick of being in bed all day long."

Jack opens his mouth as if he wants to say something, but then closes it, and turns around, walking away. I approach him and give him a hug from behind. It feels like I'm hugging a complete stranger, though. I can't shake the feeling Jack is doing his best to keep me bedbound under Misty's care. But why?

He takes my hands and slowly peels them off him. He turns around and looks at me. "I guess I can't stop you."

I get on my toes and stretch out to kiss him on the lips. "You worry too much. But I'll be fine, don't worry."

"If you say so."

I pull out my phone from my pocket, and when Jack sees what I am holding, his face turns ghost-white.

I stop what I'm doing. "Are you okay?" I ask Jack.

"Yeah, yeah." Jack nods quickly and turns around to avoid my eyes.

"I was about to call Uber. Did you...did you want to tell me something, Jack?"

"No. Not really." His voice fades away as he steps into the bathroom.

I call for Uber, ignoring this awkward exchange, and by nine, I'm already in the office.

The building looks foreign at first as I trudge on the main floor, finding my bearings. I'm wowed by the state-of-the-art facilities and feel afraid that I might not belong here. Someone appears out of nowhere and blocks my path.

"What the hell, Emily! Where have you been?"

A woman is standing in front of me, anger and confusion interlaced on her face—it's lobster red.

"Claire?" I think that's her, but reassurance doesn't hurt.

"Don't you Claire me. I've called you and texted you several times over the last two days, and you finally text me back last night while I'm sleeping? The nerve of you." Claire looks flustered, but I'm happy to see her.

I approach her and give her a big hug. "It's good to see you, Claire."

"Good to see you, too, Emily. But I won't lie. You got me worried."

"Come," I tell her.

I keep walking, glancing around as if I've never set foot here before. My steps slow as I reach the far corner, where a single door waits, my name tag centered on it like a target. This must be it.

Claire is right behind me, seemingly anxious about the explanation. "Where have you been? Are you going to tell me?"

I sit at my desk and swirl around, happy to be here. "I fell in the bathroom and had a concussion."

Claire gasps and puts her hands up on her mouth. Her eyes are as wide as a house. "Oh, my God, Emily. Are you okay now?"

I'm as calm as a cucumber. "Yeah. I'm fine." I give her a small smile. "Did I miss anything important?"

"Let's not talk about that now. Everything's under control." She pauses and gives me a smile. "I was definitely worried about you not responding."

I cock my head. "Well, thank you for saying that, Claire."

I'm afraid to tell her I have no idea where we left off or what's happening with our business.

"I would have come to visit you if I had known. But here I was thinking you took a weekend trip on a whim, like that time you went to Maine without telling me." She laughs.

I don't remember a thing about that, but I believe her.

"No." I shake my head. "I was just resting in bed."

"With all the stuff going on at home—"

Claire and I begin a staring contest. Silence lingers for long seconds.

All the stuff going on at home.

I don't know how to respond. What stuff? Is there more besides my concussion? But I can't let her know I've lost my memory. It wouldn't look good for our employees or our clients.

Or anybody.

"Right. All the stuff," I simply say.

"So, is your mother-in-law okay?"

I crease my forehead. Why is Claire asking about my mother-in-law? "Yeah, she's still in the hospital."

"Oh." Claire's voice pitches. "So, she made it to the hospital? Good for you! I'm glad it all worked out. I was a little concerned."

My mother-in-law, according to Jack, has been in the hospital since her heart surgery a few weeks ago and missed our wedding. I must have told Claire about her surgery when it happened. But I don't remember much about our conversation. It's nice of Claire to inquire about Evelyn, not that I can divulge more info. The only thing I can recall is that Evelyn had surgery and is in the hospital now. Beyond that, everything is a blur.

Claire lingers by my desk, her gaze softening. "Well, if you need anything, Emily, just let me know. We're all here for you."

I nod, forcing a smile. "Thanks, Claire. I appreciate it."

She leaves me to settle in, and I stare at my desk, the papers and files all neatly stacked as if I had never been gone. The pile looks perfect. Wow, am I really such a neat freak? What else am I going to learn about myself? I wonder. I rub my temples, trying to shake the unease crawling beneath my skin.

I can't help but question myself: Who am I, and what kind of mysterious triangle have I gotten myself into?

Everything feels like a big fat lie. How do I reach the truth?

CHAPTER 36

Jack

AS SOON AS Emily leaves the house, I pound on Misty's door. "Open the fucking door, Misty."

Why is she locked in there?

The door swings wide open, and Misty stands there, leaning on the cane, looking content. I wonder if she's faking her need for the cane, just as she exaggerated the severity of her fall. She's absolutely twisted.

"Yes, Jack? How can I help you?"

I can't contain my anger. "I've told you to keep Emily away from her phone, and look what you've done."

"What have I done?" Sarcasm seeps out of her voice.

"You let her wander around the house until she found her phone. That's what you've done!"

I walk past Misty and enter the bedroom, pacing back and forth.

"So what, Jack? So what if Emily found her phone?"

I halt my pacing and look at her, daggers shooting from my eyes. "Stop fucking with me. You've already done enough. You know, if her memory returns, we're both screwed."

"Not necessarily," she says playfully.

"What do you mean?"

"Emily doesn't need to find out shit if you get moving." She claps her hands twice and raises her voice. "Chop, chop, Jack. The sooner you do me this one favor, the sooner you're off the hook. Both you and your wife. Do you get it? We don't want to drag this on forever."

I stand there, contemplating what she's saying. I don't think I have a choice at this point. Misty needs to get out of this house and my life and never be seen again.

But she's already taken steps to sabotage me and share my darkest secret with Emily.

"I found an old polaroid photo of me from the accident in the half bathroom downstairs. Where did it come from? Did you give it to Emily?" I press further. If Emily ever discovers the hit-and-run, she'll never trust me again. She'll divorce me, no doubt, and take everything with her. Worse, it will destroy my career, ruin my reputation as a lawyer, and leave me with nothing.

After I've worked so hard to upend my life and change for the better.

How could I possibly explain to Emily—or anyone—that the accident happened during one of the lowest, most vulnerable times of my life? I was young, reckless, and thought that drowning my problems in alcohol would somehow solve everything. That night, I was leaving a party, drunk and completely out of control. I didn't even see the woman crossing the street until it was too late. Who would expect someone to be walking around at that hour, past midnight? The streets were supposed to be empty.

When I hit her, everything inside me shut down. The panic was overwhelming. My heart was pounding in my chest, my hands were shaking. Instead of stopping, instead of helping, I did the unthinkable. I fled. I couldn't face the consequences. I left her there, lying on the road, and sped away like a coward.

Now, years later, the guilt still lingers, always threatening to resurface. How could I ever tell Emily? She'd never forgive me. She'd see me for what I truly am—weak, selfish. If she knew the truth, it would all be over.

No one would feel sympathy for the murderer.

Misty snaps her head and gasps hard. "The photo? Are you kiddin' me?" She seems genuinely confused. "Why would you accuse me of such a thing, Jack? Besides, haven't you seen me lying in your fucking bed for days, unable to move? How could I have done it?"

"Well, you could have hired someone, Misty. And I think you're very capable of doing it."

"You know what? Fuck you, Jack. If I wanted to blackmail you, I'd have done it a while ago."

I smirk and look at her. "So why didn't you?"

"You really know why? I'm not here to destroy your marriage. Besides, Emily seems like a lovely person. She doesn't deserve a home wrecker."

"Since when do you care about Emily?" I'm disgusted with her. She's such a snake.

She chuckles. "Fine. I don't care about her as much as you'd think, but honest to God, I don't give two shits about your marriage. I just need you to do me the favor, Jack. How many fucking times do I need to say it? What are you waiting for?"

"For one, you're asking me to do something illegal. If I get caught, I'm going to lose my bar license."

She crosses her arms over her torso. "And? You didn't seem to be concerned about my bar license when I got you off after your hit and run."

I roll my eyes and huff. Jesus. Arguing with another lawyer is the worst. Pointless.

"Alright. I'll do it. But as soon as I'm finished, you're out of this home, and I never want to see you again. You get it?"

Misty chuckles softly again. She really knows how to enrage me. "The feeling is mutual, dear. Or should I call you...my son?" She laughs, then instantly becomes serious. "How long will it take?"

"I will be done soon. Like in the next twenty-four hours." A lot will have to go into preparation for doing her this favor, and she should be damn grateful. "And then you leave my home for good. Got that?"

Misty nods and smiles. "The pleasure is all mine."

I storm out of the room, slamming the door behind me. My heart pounds in my chest as I realize there's no way out of this without crossing yet another line. But once Misty is gone, maybe—just maybe—I'll finally get a chance to fix the mess I've made.

CHAPTER 37

Emily

I COME HOME and find Misty in the living room, watching TV. She's the last person I want to see when I arrive home. She just rubs me the wrong way with that creepy smile of hers. As the clock ticks, her familiarity surfaces more and more—I've seen her somewhere before, but I just don't remember the details.

Misty shoots me a quick look over her shoulder before she goes back to staring at the screen. "Feeling any better?"

"Yeah. Thanks." I'm short. I don't feel like exchanging niceties. At this point, I just want to know when she is going to leave.

"Oh, good." She sounds delighted.

I sit across from her and give her a good stare. She does a double take until her eyes land on me. "Yes?"

"Misty." I lean forward and place my elbows on my lap. "I appreciate you taking care of me the past two days. But I think I'm almost fully recovered. If you want to go home, you should."

"You're fully recovered? Are you sure?"

Physically, I feel a lot better. Mentally, I am still waiting for all my memories to come back. But I don't tell her that. Instead, I'm curt. "Yes. Very much so."

She nods. "Well, I was planning on leaving tomorrow, anyway."

"You were?"

"Absolutely. My job here's done." She smiles, then goes back to watching TV.

Later that evening, when I talk to Jack, I relay what Misty told me: tomorrow is the day she leaves.

When Jack hears, he rubs his neck and fidgets around, as if doing his best to abate his concern. What is he concerned about?

"She said that?" he finally says.

I nod. "Yeah. That's okay, right? I mean, I'm fine now. I don't need anyone's supervision. In fact, I did quite well at work today...with Claire and all." I swallow as I think about how hard it was to remember who Claire was and to reorient myself at work earlier.

He creases his brows as he looks at me. "That's good, honey." He comes near and kisses me on the head. "That's great."

As he moves away, I can't help but sense anxiety enveloping Jack. One thing I remember about Jack is that he's been always so positive and joyous, but now, he seems like a bundle of nerves. In fact, we don't snuggle anymore like we used to. The warmth and easy affection we once shared have been replaced by tension, as if he's constantly on edge. I watch him move through the house, his shoulders hunched, his movements jerky, like he's carrying some invisible weight. I want to ask him what's wrong, to confront the distance growing between us, but something holds me back—fear, maybe. Or the gnawing suspicion that whatever's troubling him is something he's not ready, or willing, to share with me.

He's so on edge he can't sleep. Slipping out of bed slowly, he moves carefully, as if hoping not to wake me. But my headache has returned, pounding away, despite the four ibuprofen I took earlier, keeping me wide awake.

When Jack exits the bedroom, I gaze at the alarm clock. It's past midnight. Jack is probably thirsty and has gone to the kitchen to get himself a glass of water.

Shortly after, however, I hear the front door slam echoing along the house. I jolt out of bed and run to the window to see Jack on the curb, rushing toward the Prudential Center. Where's he going?

I'm inclined to follow him, but I won't be able to catch up to him. Is this something Jack has always done, but I just don't remember? Maybe he couldn't sleep and had decided to take a brisk walk around the neighborhood until he got that extra energy out of his system?

I stand by the window, watching Jack disappear into the night, uncertainty twisting in my gut. His late-night walks don't feel familiar, but with so many memories still missing, I can't trust my instincts. I sit on the edge of the bed, feeling the headache pulsating at my temples, the pressure building behind my eyes.

I try to reason with myself—maybe Jack really is just restless, maybe work has him stressed—but the longer I sit there, the more my doubts creep in. Jack isn't acting like himself, and now, sneaking out in the middle of the night? It doesn't add up.

Minutes pass. I glance at the door, considering whether I should wait for him to return. But the thought of just sitting here in silence with my thoughts is unbearable. I need answers, and I can't get them by staying here.

I slip out of the bedroom, careful not to make any noise. The house feels eerily quiet—Misty must be in a deep sleep. I plod through the hallway, my heart pounding as I head toward the front door. The air outside is cold, sharp against my skin, but it jolts me awake, clearing some of the fog that has clouded my mind. I glance in the direction Jack went, but he's long gone, swallowed by the city's dark streets. There's no point in me chasing him.

I shove my hands in my pockets, shivering in the cold, feeling the weight of my phone. Maybe I should call him or track his location—anything to figure out where he went and why. But something stops me. I hesitate, my thumb hovering over the screen, unsure of what I'd even say. Do I really want to know what he's doing, or do I prefer the comfort of ignorance?

The answer feels obvious, but the fear lingers.

I head back inside, closing the door quietly behind me. My heart is still racing, and now, I feel like I've stepped into a darker place. Jack's anxiety, his late-night excursions, the strange dynamic between him and Misty—it all feels like pieces of a puzzle I can't quite fit together.

I move back toward the bedroom, passing Misty's door. My steps falter when I hear a sound from the inside—a soft murmur, followed by what sounds like movement. I freeze, my breath catching in my throat. She's awake?

Curiosity and suspicion surge inside me, and before I can stop myself, I press my ear against the door, straining to hear. I catch bits and pieces. Misty is whispering, her voice low and sharp. It sounds like she's on the phone.

"...he's out...I don't know how much longer I can keep this up...no, she still doesn't remember..."

My stomach knots. She must be talking about Jack. And me. I want to burst through the door and confront Misty, but fear coils in my gut, freezing me in place. My body feels weak, my knees unsteady—I doubt I could even lift a finger. There has to be another way.

I back away from the door, careful not to make a sound. Whatever is happening, Misty and Jack are hiding something from me. I need to find out what—before it's too late.

CHAPTER 38

Jack

IT'S DONE.

As I hurry home, I can't stop thinking about what I've just done. I feel sick to my stomach.

Tampering with evidence is a federal crime. If I get caught, I won't just face prison time; I'll also lose my bar license and never practice law again. Misty has gotten herself in trouble for tax evasion, and she's asked me to help her out of this mess. Otherwise, she could end up behind bars.

There are two certainties in life: taxes and death, both of which Misty has avoided.

But Misty is clear that I owe her a favor from years ago when she got me off the hit-and-run charges. None of this feels right, but I don't have a choice. It's the only way to get rid of her and preserve my life.

As soon as I arrive home, I march into Misty's bedroom. It's way past two a.m. and the house is quiet, as it should be. I only hope Emily is in dreamland and can't hear anything.

As I expected, Misty was wide awake, waiting for my report. She sits in the chair by the window, cloaked in darkness, her face barely illuminated by the faint glow of the streetlights outside. She looks like a doll set out for display. I think I catch a hint of a smile cracking across her face—but in the shadows, I can't be certain.

"Hi, Jack." She's whispering, and I get why. It wouldn't be good if we woke up Emily.

The silhouette of her arm moves up and reaches for the lamp. The bright light makes me squint. It's too much for this late at night. I should sleep now, for Christ's sake.

Misty is sitting in her pajamas, looking relaxed. She has that same look she gets whenever she feels like she's just gotten away with something, and I was the one who helped her pull it off. Disgust churns inside me. She raises her brows, waiting for me to speak up, to confirm it all.

"It's done," I tell her. In the heat of the moment, I feel anger, guilt, relief all at once.

She nods slowly while staring at me. "Great job, Jack. So, when I wake up, my records will look different? All the evidence will play in my favor?"

I smirk. I hate myself for being that guy, but what choice did I have? "Yes," I say through my clenched teeth.

She lets out a silent laugh. "Excellent. Now we're even—as far as favors go."

"We are. Now, I can only hope you will be gone tomorrow, first thing in the morning, and I'll never see you again."

Her face turns serious. "Not so fast, Jacky boy."

I snap, feeling the air rush out of me. "What?"

"I have one more thing to do before I disappear from your life."

I want to scream, but I don't want to wake up Emily. "What the fuck do you mean?" I ask in a loud whisper, anger boiling inside me. I'm doing my best to contain my rage and not fall into her trap.

Again.

Misty leans back in her chair, her smile widening as she sees the tension radiating off me. "I told you I'd leave, Jack. And I will," she says, her voice almost too calm. "But not before you do something else."

My hands clench into fists, but I force myself to stay calm. "And what exactly is that? You've already dragged me back into this mess. What more could you possibly want?"

She tilts her head, studying me like I'm some puzzle she's still working out. "It's simple, Jack."

I shake my head, exasperated. "You've got your clean record now. What else could you want from me?"

She stands slowly, crossing the room until she's just inches from me, her eyes dark and menacing. "I want you to leave Emily."

My stomach drops, the weight of her words hitting me like a punch to the gut. I don't think I'm hearing correctly. "What? Where is this coming from all of a sudden?" I whisper, my voice shaking with barely contained fury.

Misty's smile fades, replaced by something colder, more dangerous. "I know you don't like surprises. I remember that from back in the day. But I don't want to hurt her, Jack. I just need her...gone. Far enough away that she can't interfere with anything."

I grit my teeth, feeling the rage boil just beneath the surface. "You leave her out of this, Misty. She's done nothing to you."

Her gaze hardens. "It's not that. You fucking know you don't deserve her."

I can feel my control slipping, the walls closing in. I've already done too much, crossed too many lines for Misty. But this? Why does she need Emily gone? This is something I can't do.

"I won't," I hiss, stepping back from her. "You can take your threats and get out of my life for good. I won't let you manipulate me anymore."

She stares at me, her expression unreadable. For a

moment, there's a tense silence between us, the air thick with unsaid words.

Finally, she lets out a sigh, a small, almost disappointed smile tugging at her lips. "Suit yourself, Jack. But remember —if you won't get rid of her, I will."

CHAPTER 39

Emily

THE IMAGE of Jack disappearing into the night in the wee hours flashes in front of my eyes. I was asleep when Jack returned to bed, so I have no way of knowing how long he was away. Jack stands up and goes to the bathroom, closing the door behind him.

The doorbell rings downstairs, leaving me stunned. We don't have many visitors, much less ones that ring the door-bell. I didn't even know what it sounded like until today.

I get up and look through the window and crane my neck. I see a person—a man—standing at the door.

"Emily!" Jack yells from behind the bathroom door. "Can you get that, please?"

"Of course."

As I walk to the door, the bell rings once again, sending an eerie chill into the house. I pass by the guest room, which is shut tight. Misty must be still sleeping. Though I imagine she will be packing her stuff, since she's leaving today.

I open the door to greet a middle-aged man. I don't think I've seen him before, but then...my memory. Unexpected visits make me nervous, and I tend to think the worst.

"Hi, how are you? I'm your next-door neighbor, Scott. Nice to meet you."

I sigh in relief. I definitely haven't seen him before. "Oh. Hi. I'm Emily Ross."

"Listen, I don't want to alarm you, but I think the flood in your house caused some damage to the wall in my hallway."

I crease my brows, confused. "Flood?"

"Didn't you guys have a flood recently? I'm pretty sure I saw people coming in and out a few days ago to fix it."

I don't want to appear like I don't know what he's talking about. I'll need to ask Jack about this. But not to be dismissive, I must think quick on my feet. "I'm so sorry to hear this. Why don't you take photos of the damage and send them to us? We'll file a case through our insurance company."

He doesn't look pleased, even though I'm offering a solution. I don't blame him—any disturbance is disruptive.

"I can do that." He scratches his face while gazing at the ground. Then he looks at me with his squinty eyes and proceeds, "I hate to broach this subject, but while I'm here, can I also ask you and your husband to keep it quiet while you argue? You know, I could hear almost everything from my bedroom when you guys were fighting this morning at two a.m."

My memory has been brittle lately, but I don't remember arguing with Jack at all. All I remember is that he left the house in the middle of the night and returned God knows when.

"Oh, gosh. I'm so sorry about that."

Scott gives me a tight smile, though I can tell an apology isn't enough. "It's okay, just...you know, thin walls."

"Of course," I reply, feeling a knot of anxiety tighten in my stomach. "I'll make sure it doesn't happen again."

He nods, then turns to leave, but not before giving me another lingering glance. I close the door slowly, leaning against it for a moment as I try to process what he said. A flood? Arguing? None of it makes any sense. I don't remember any of that happening. My memory feels like a fragile thread, and it's becoming harder to distinguish what's real and what isn't.

I head back upstairs, my mind racing. Jack is still in the bathroom. I sit on the edge of the bed, getting ready to face Jack. What if Scott wasn't exaggerating? What if Jack and I really did argue, and I just...forgot? The thought unsettles me more than I'd like to admit.

Jack emerges from the bathroom, a towel draped around his shoulders. He smiles at me. "Who was that?"

"Our neighbor," I say carefully, watching his reaction. "Scott. He mentioned a flood in the house?"

Jack pauses, his expression neutral. "Oh, right! There was a small issue with the plumbing earlier this week. It's all fixed now."

I nod, not entirely convinced. "He also said...he heard us arguing last night."

Jack raises an eyebrow. "Arguing? We didn't argue, Em."

I hesitate, unsure of myself. "He seemed pretty confident about it."

Jack chuckles lightly, shaking his head. "He's mistaken. We didn't fight."

I stare at him for a long moment, searching his face for any sign that he's hiding something. But Jack remains calm, collected, as if nothing is wrong. He makes a beeline for the dresser and pulls out fresh underwear.

His calmness does little to inspire confidence. "Okay. Was it you and Misty that argued?"

Jack turns around to face me. "Emily! What makes you say that? No one was arguing. The guy was probably hallucinating."

"Jack..."

He scoffs and sighs. "Okay. I guess we did argue. I asked Misty to leave today because she was hesitant at first. She thinks you're still not well enough and need care."

"Oh." I'm shocked to hear this. "I can talk to Misty again and ask her to leave. Okay, honey?"

I stand up with renewed energy and approach Jack to give him a kiss. He seems just as anxious as I am for Misty to leave.

When I knock on her door, she doesn't answer. I reach for the doorknob and twist it, slowly opening the door, calling for Misty. I look around, only seeing empty space. I step inside and proceed to the bathroom, still finding nothing or nobody.

I go downstairs in case she's watching TV or eating breakfast, but the kitchen and living room are empty. With the lonesome humming sound of the fridge, the house has a certain tranquil quality to it on an easy morning.

I call her name. "Misty! Misty?" She could be in the downstairs half-bathroom, but the door is wide open, and the lights are off. No Misty. The humming sound persists.

That's when it hits me—Misty is gone.

<h1>CHAPTER 40</h1>

Emily

I GO UPSTAIRS to tell Jack Misty is gone. He says, "It's impossible. Her luggage is still sitting on the floor. Unless she left without it?"

I shrug. "I don't know, Jack. I don't know anything anymore." Anger rises inside of me. "Listen, I know I've suffered a concussion recently, but all these things happening with Misty and now the neighbor and everything else...nothing makes sense, Jack. And I feel like you're not telling me something I should know. Something very important. What is it? Tell me!" I'm nearly screaming.

"Calm down, Emily."

"Don't tell me to calm down!" I scream at the top of my lungs. And that's ironic. But he should know it's a vicious cycle. The more you tell your wife to relax, the more she becomes enraged.

Jack is stunned. He swallows hard and nods quickly. "Emily. Listen. How about we take time out and start again? Misty will be gone today, and we can resume our happy life again. Maybe we can take another quick trip somewhere? Maine or Vermont? What do you think?"

I'm too angry to think so I tell him, "I'll think about it. I'm going for a walk now to clear my head."

"Okay, that sounds like a good plan, honey." Jack looks pleased. He leans forward to kiss me, but I jerk away and head for the door.

"When I return, you'd better have some answers for me." My voice is sharp. "Because I'm sick of the unknowns, Jack."

With that, I slam the door behind me. But that echoing sound feels like a sign—a sign that I am close to finding the truth.

CHAPTER 41

Jack

It's time to confess everything. It's time to sit down with Emily and have a real talk. It's the time to get our life back. I really hope everything will turn out okay.

CHAPTER 42

Emily

I DON'T REMEMBER the last time I was this angry.

All my past frustrations are manifesting themselves into a fast walk. My fists clench, and my breath quickens as I weave through the crowd, hardly noticing the people I brush past. It's like all the resentment I've kept bottled up is finally spilling over, driving me forward with a single focus—getting answers. The city around me blurs into the background, and all I can feel is the heat of my anger pulsing through me with every step.

It's painfully clear that Jack is hiding something from me, and Misty has to be involved. A chill of fear creeps in—I don't even know if I'm safe. What is Misty capable of? Why is she here? Who is she, really? I'd never even heard of her before now, and I can't shake the feeling there's a hidden reason for her visit. Anger simmers under my skin, and I want to punch the air just to release it.

When I get onto Boylston Street, the flood of car sounds awakens my senses. I'm more alert and, at the moment, feel alive. It's like something invisible is nudging me and telling me to snap out of it and get a grip on my life.

Driven forward by adrenaline, I look ahead until I pass a cafe on the other side of the street. A woman, who looks awfully familiar, is sitting at a table. I squint to check who she is. I've seen her many times before.

Jenna. My bestie from college.

She's sitting with company and having a cup of coffee and a croissant. It's so good to see a familiar face in the heart of the city, though I guess it's not so unusual to see Jenna since she practically lives around the corner.

I halt in the middle of the curb and wait for the cars to pass so I can cross the street and join Jenna and her friend. But as I wait for the cars to pass, I take a better look at her friend and gasp when I see Misty sitting next to her.

What is Misty doing with Jenna? Do they know each other?

As I study their expressions, a chill runs down my spine. Jenna looks tense, leaning in close to Misty, who appears calm, too calm, with that same eerie smile that has unsettled me since she first arrived at my house. But it's not just that.

Something about her posture, the way she holds herself—it's all wrong. And then, like a bolt of lightning, the memory slams into me.

I remember now perfectly that Misty came to our house, but not as Misty. She's an imposter, pretending to be Jack's mother, Evelyn.

Memories are flooding me like a storm on a sunny day. My real mother-in-law is in the hospital, and now I remember calling a Seattle hospital confirming this before I had that concussion.

Oh... my... God.

Everything becomes so clear, like someone spelled it out for me. It makes sense—the fact that Misty and Jack don't resemble each other at all. Or that, even if she really was Jack's mother, she would do a better job of not making him scrambled eggs when he clearly hates them. Or that she looks a lot younger than she should be for a middle-aged woman. All the awkward conversations and interactions—I was so naïve to believe it all.

But still—this doesn't explain why or how she is connected to Jenna. And what about Jack? Why hadn't he told me that Evelyn wasn't really his mother, but someone entirely unknown to me?

Jack hasn't changed a bit. I should have known better.

They are clearly in it together—whatever it is.

I feel dizzy. My heart pounds as the realization sinks in.

Misty hadn't come to help me recover—her reasons have to be far more sinister. And Jack... Jack must have known. He had to know.

The cars rush past me, but all I can hear is the sound of my heartbeat in my ears. I step back from the curb, unable to move forward. Misty laughs lightly at something Jenna says, but I know the truth now. That laugh, that smile—they're all part of the mask she's been wearing.

I turn away quickly, not wanting to be seen, and head back in the direction I came from, my mind racing. If Misty is here, first pretending to be Evelyn, then acting like she was my caregiver, everything that has happened over the last week is a big, fat lie. But why? What does she want from me?

As I walk, my thoughts swirl like a storm, and one thing becomes clear—I need to confront Jack. I need answers, and I need them now.

CHAPTER 43

Jack

THINGS HAVE GONE WAY OUT of control. Emily demands answers, and I need to be ready. I should confess and tell her everything: that I killed someone in a hit-and-run when I drove drunk ten years ago and got away with it. That Misty helped me get away with it. That she was pretending to be my mother, the only way to worm into our lives. That Misty came for a payback.

But I can't tell her that Misty has more in store for us.

She's asking me to leave Emily, and if I don't...I don't know what she will do, and I'm afraid to imagine. Misty is crazy, and she's got no remorse. It implies she won't leave until she's even.

Shit shit shit.

How did I get myself into this mess?

I had to leave the house to clear my head and figure out my next move. I walk in a direction I'm certain will keep me from crossing paths with Emily, who's out walking, too.

Gosh, we used to take these afternoon walks together every weekend, like it was the best thing in the world. We would appreciate our companionship of discovering new things, visiting cafes along the way, learning about one another. Can we ever go back to our normal selves?

Misty is to blame for everything, but I can't blame her completely. I haven't been honest with my wife. I haven't told her everything about me, including my darkest secret.

I'm so consumed by thoughts and guilt that I'm barely paying attention to my surroundings. My feet automatically take me home, my mind churning with what I'm about to say to Emily. I'm going to tell her the truth and apologize.

I slow down as I approach our building. My heart is pounding in my chest as I picture an enraged Emily seeking an explanation. But something seems strange about the house. The blinds are down, and nothing can be seen from the outside. Our brownstone townhouse looks abandoned, as if haunted by demons.

I approach the door, place the key in the keyhole, but the door won't budge. I lean back to check if I might be mistaken and come to the wrong place, but no...it says 34 Newbury Street.

Uneasiness grows as I attempt to open the door, and pedestrians give me a funny stare, as if I'm breaking in. My next option is the doorbell, so I reluctantly push the button, waiting for someone to open the door.

Nothing.

I turn around and bury my face in the door, peeking through the double-pain window, searching for life inside. It's adorned with a colorful design, so it's difficult to see anything. Just as I'm about to lift my arm and start banging the shit out of it, the door opens. On the other side, Emily stands with her long hair let down and messy. Her eyes are shooting daggers at me, yet she's wearing an evil smile that sends shivers down my spine.

"Emily," I gasp, though I am not sure if I'm happy or not to see her. Not like this.

"Hello, Jack." Her voice sounds distorted, like it doesn't belong to her. Emily doesn't look like the same charming woman I've learned to love and appreciate.

She looks like a menace. Like someone coming out of a horror movie.

"What...what happened to the door?" I chuckle nervously as I lift the key in the air.

Her smile grows wider and more eerie. "You surely found a miracle worker, Jack. I have Peter on speed dial now. He came over and changed the lock in a jiffy."

I sigh in relief. "Oh, that. That's great."

I'm assuming she did it to shield our home from the intruder and the imposter, Misty. Why didn't I think of that sooner? Though I am still uncertain if Emily's memory has been restored. Would she know that Evelyn and Misty are the same person?

If she doesn't, she will soon. I intend to tell her everything.

We stand there for what seems like eternity until she says, "Would you like to come in, Jack?"

"Yeah, Emily. I'd love to."

Progress.

She slowly takes a couple of steps back to allow me in. Her eyes follow me as I slowly make my way in. The place looks like a dungeon: dark and uninviting, with all the blinds covering the windows. It's silent except for the mumbling in a near distance I can't quite decipher.

Emily is right behind me, shuffling her feet. "Come on, Jack. Don't be afraid. Keep walking."

Afraid? Why would I be afraid?

But soon it becomes clear. On the kitchen floor, there are two individuals with their hands and feet tied; their mouths secured shut with duct tape. The better I look, the more it becomes clear. The two individuals sitting on my kitchen floor are Misty and Jenna.

CHAPTER 44

Jack

"WHAT IS HAPPENING HERE?" I'm out of breath as I watch the two helpless women fight to free themselves.

"Is it not obvious, Jack?"

Emily's voice is crisp as ice.

As I watch Jenna and Misty struggle, something in the apartment strikes me as odd. As my senses sharpen, I hear the classical music playing in the background. Vivaldi's *The Four Seasons*. Emily knows well the sound of a violin makes my skin crawl.

"What... what is this nonsense, Emily?" I'm alluding to the music that's driving me to a mental abyss. When I turn around to face Emily, I see something in her hand. I do a double take when I notice she's holding a gun. "Emily, is that a gun?"

The annoyance of the music is replaced by a rush of fear.

"What does it look like?" Emily smirks.

The muffled commotion from the two women increases as they see Emily pointing the gun at me.

"Take it easy, darling," I tell her, but it falls on deaf ears.

"Sit down, Jack. And don't call me darling. You know I always hated that word."

"Fine. I'm sorry. I won't call you that again."

"Sit down, I said." She raises her voice, anger projecting from her.

I approach the closest chair and plop down like someone violently pushed me.

"What is this all about? I see you got Misty and Jenna. What are you planning to do with them?"

How had she got both captured at the same time? Emily is totally mad and unhinged. Plus, what is the endgame here? She needs to explain herself.

"I'm not planning on doing anything with them. It's all going to be you." She laughs.

"What?"

"Before we get into the nitty-gritty, you should know that you've missed a nice chat with these two ladies. You want to hear?"

I nod. But I'm not sure I do. With the gun in her hand, I

don't think it's a good idea to refuse anything Emily suggests. "Of course. Please tell me."

"Where do I even begin?"

For dramatic effect, Emily looks up at the ceiling and puts her hand up to her chin as if she's thinking hard.

"Let's start with Jenna. Supposedly my bestie." She gazes in her direction and scoffs. "Did you know the bitch has been drooling over you since the night we all met?"

Well, yes, I've always known, but I'm afraid to admit that right now. I put my head down, avoiding Emily's eyes.

"You knew it, didn't you, Jack?"

"I did, but it meant nothing, Emily. I've always wanted you."

"Whatever. I don't give a shit. You probably deserve each other."

My head snaps back, as I am not sure what Emily means. I remain silent, not wishing to incriminate myself further.

"Did you know Misty stalked me before she came to Boston and found Jenna among my friends on Instagram? And this bitch, supposedly my best friend, gave our home address to the imposter? I mean, what the fuck? I guess she wanted you this bad."

"That's terrible," I say to appease Emily. "I wasn't sure how Misty got our home address, but now it's clear." I look in their direction; Jenna's eyes appear remorseful while Misty is shooting daggers from hers. "I see why you'd be mad, Emily. They played us well."

"Shut the hell up, Jack!" Emily yells. "I didn't tell you to speak, did I?"

She points the gun at me, leaving me speechless. She's more than angry—she's completely unraveling.

"Emily, listen," I start, trying to keep my voice calm. "This doesn't have to go any further. Let's just talk, okay? We can figure this out together."

She laughs bitterly, the sound cold and detached. "Oh, Jack. We're way past talking. And I don't really care for your lies." Her voice is sharp. "For years, I've been played by everyone around me. But no more. Today, things change."

I glance at Jenna and Misty, both squirming, their eyes wide with fear. I need to find a way to de-escalate this before someone gets hurt. My mind races, but I keep my voice steady. "Emily, you don't want to do this. Think about what comes next."

"What comes next?" Emily says, her voice dangerously quiet. She tightens her grip on the gun. "You're going to make things right, Jack. I'm tired of being manipulated, tired of people like you lying to my face."

Her words hit me like a punch. I never meant for things to go this far—never. All that has happened was the attempt of self-preservation that didn't quite pan out. I should have been honest with Emily from the very beginning. It's the price I'm now going to pay.

I'm not the one holding the cards anymore. Emily is. And she's determined to take back control.

"What do you want me to do? I'll do anything to make things better," I ask, keeping my hands where she can see them.

She steps closer, her eyes narrowing. "I'll make it easy for you, Jack. You'll help get rid of Misty and Jenna before you get rid of yourself."

My heart stops. I stare at Emily in disbelief, but she's dead serious. The air in the room feels unbearable, the classical music in the background suddenly haunting. Vivaldi's violin screeches in the air, making me feel like I'm trapped in a nightmare.

"I—I can't," I stammer.

Emily's eyes harden. "You will. Or I'll choose for you. And I promise, Jack, you won't like the outcome."

The room spins as the reality of the situation crashes down on me. I glance at Jenna, her face pale and terrified, then at Misty, whose expression remains defiant, cold. There has to be a way out of this, some way to stop Emily before it's too late.

But as I sit there, paralyzed with fear, I realize that no matter what choice I make, nothing will ever be the same again.

Emily

JACK IS STARING at me with gigantic eyes, fear emanating from them.

I, on the other hand, feel calm. I'm sitting across from him, about to deliver the last piece of news none of them know about me.

I take the photo out of my back pocket of my jeans and wave at him. "Remember this dreadful day, Jack?"

He leans forward and squints to see what I'm holding. "What is that?"

"Does the name Grace Holloway ring a bell?"

Jack opens his eyes and mouth wide. He's speechless. The mumbling in the kitchen goes wilder—it must be Misty who's just as shocked to hear the name.

"What happened, Jack? A cat got your tongue?"

He's still staring at me in disbelief.

"You see this photo?" I point it at him, so he can see better. "It's the photo of you and me. When we first met."

"What...what do you mean?" Jack stammers.

A sour smile forms on my lips. "It just happens that I'm no longer Grace Holloway." I pause. "I'd changed my name to Emily."

When he realizes what I'm holding, his eyes bulge. "It can't be."

"Oh. Yeah. I forgot to tell you another piece of info. My bestie here, Jenna, sent this photo, hoping to raise awareness that you've murdered someone years ago. She was hoping, once I knew you were the murderer, I would leave you, and she would just slide into your life. She had no idea I already knew what you'd done."

Mumbling in the kitchen amplifies.

Jack stares at me, a lump slowly traveling down his neck.

I gaze at the photo, then back at him. "It's the day of the accident, Jack. It's the day you left me for the dead on the road, like I was a squirrel."

A large lump forms in my throat. My memory hasn't always served me well, but I do recall the haze and confusion as I emerged from my coma. It was relearning everything about who I am and the world around me. Not to mention all the lost time I'd never get back. I was in my twenties, the prime time to feel youth, yet I had to navigate this new reality like an infant while my perpetrator remained out there, still free and unpunished.

I do my best to stifle a cry.

"I don't understand." Jack looks shocked.

"Oh, of course you don't, Jack. It's because both you and your friend here thought you'd killed your hit-and-run. But guess what? I made it. After you hit me with your car and ran away, a man found me on the edge of the road and took me to the hospital. I survived. Something you and your friend here didn't know."

I gaze at the ladies on the floor, and Misty looks shocked, too. She's mumbling something through duct tape, none of it discernable.

"I know," I continue. "It's shocking to hear, isn't it? You sent me into a coma for months. Doctors didn't think I was going to make it. But miracles do fucking happen, Jack. And then I had to find you. And I'm so glad I did."

I let out a loud, involuntary laugh. Jack slumps in his chair, barely moving.

"If it wasn't for Misty, my plan would have been different to make you pay, but she showed up out of nowhere and did the job for me. She dug your grave, nice and deep." I turn in her direction and say sarcastically, "Thanks, Misty. You're a doll."

Jack looks confused.

"She told me all about her tax evasion problems, and you helped her. Well, your career is over, my friend. And everything you have, you can wave it goodbye."

Jack looks like he's about to cry.

"On the positive side, though... aren't you happy to know you didn't kill me? Relieved to know you're not a murderer, after all?"

Jack says nothing; he just keeps staring.

"What kind of person hits another human in a car and runs away?" My teeth are clenched, my anger unhinged. "You're a disgusting human being, if that's what I can call you. And now all the lies about your friend Misty? You were both in on it, pretending she was your mother."

Jack lowers his gaze and shakes his head. He's been caught with his pants down.

"What do you want from me now?" Jack whimpers.

"We're impatient, aren't we?"

I stand up and go to the kitchen, keeping an eye out on Jack. I retrieve the biggest knife there is and shuffle to Jack and hand it to him. "Get going, Jack. We don't have all day."

Jack stares at the knife, his hand trembling as he reluctantly takes it from me. His eyes dart between Misty, Jenna, and me, desperation clear on his face. The weight of his actions—the accident, the lies, the abandonment—I can see the fear twisting inside him.

"Emily," he pleads, his voice cracking. "Please, let's not do this. We can figure something out."

I shake my head slowly, a smirk playing on my lips. "There's nothing to figure out. You need to pay for what you did."

The silence in the room is deafening. Misty's muffled cries grow louder behind the duct tape, and Jenna's eyes are wide with horror, though she doesn't make a sound. The tension is thick, suffocating, as Jack remains frozen in place, the knife hanging limply in his hand.

"You made your choice the day you left me there to die. You think you made yourself a better person over the years? You think you can just slap lipstick on a pig and make it look pretty?" Jack looks at me, confused.

"Yes, you're the pig!" I yell. "And you're still that same bad person from years ago."

A violin screeches in the background. Jack looks completely spent.

I continue, "And look, you still make terrible choices in life." My voice cracks. "You're the last person I could ever trust."

"So, you never loved me?" Jack almost cries.

For a split second, I feel sorry for him. "Love you? Jack…"

Jack's grip tightens on the knife, his knuckles white. He looks at me, searching my face for any hint of mercy, but I give him none. He glances at Jenna, then at Misty, his face contorted in agony as he realizes what I'm asking him to do.

"You want me to—" Jack's voice falters. "Emily, I can't."

"You can," I snap, my calm demeanor cracking slightly. "And you will."

Jack's eyes well with tears, his chest rising and falling with shallow breaths. He glances at the women again, shaking his head and sweating profusely.

"There's no way out of this. You've already crossed the line, and now you need to finish what you started."

The knife in his hand wavers. He looks back at me, eyes full of regret, before he falls to his knees, the knife clattering to the floor beside him.

"I can't do this," Jack whispers, broken. "I can't."

I expect more of a fight, more resistance, but all I see is the shell of a man who knows he's lost.

I step forward, standing over him, my eyes burning with years of pent-up rage. "Pathetic," I whisper, more to myself than to him.

I pick up the knife, and Jack looks up at me, a flicker of fear returning to his eyes as I grip the handle tightly.

"I wanted you to suffer," I whisper. "To feel what I felt all those years ago. But now I see...you're already suffering enough."

I lower the knife, letting it fall to the ground with a dull thud.

"Get out," I tell him, my voice cold and empty. "Take them with you. And never come back."

Jack's breath catches in his throat, his eyes widening in disbelief. "Emily—"

"Get out!" I shout, stepping back, pointing toward the door. "Before I change my mind."

Without another word, Jack scrambles to his feet. He rushes to untie Misty and Jenna, his hands shaking as he frees them. They stumble to the door, all three of them hurrying out as quickly as they can, not daring to look back. I quietly close the door and turn the lock. With the new lock in place, Jack won't be able to get back in.

And just like that, the apartment falls silent, save for the screech of a distant violin. I sink onto the couch, drained, letting the gun slip from my hand with a satisfied smile. It's just a cheap plastic toy I picked up at a store, but it looks authentic enough to put a terror in Jack's eyes. The image in my head makes me laugh.

If he only knew.

But thank goodness, it's all over now. I feel nothing short of relief when I realize there will be no more lies, no more deceit.

Hands down, one of the best days of my life.

CHAPTER 46

One Month Later

SEATTLE IS ENCHANTING IN AUTUMN. The sun sparkles on the ocean, casting glimmers on the water, with the city skyline rising prominently in the foreground. The Space Needle stands tall against the sky, evoking a cascade of memories from the days I spent wandering the city, seeking refuge from my troubles. Even from a distance, boats bob on gentle waves, their hulls shimmering in the sunlight, awakening a sense of nostalgia.

For the long Labor Day weekend, I'm visiting my old stomping grounds where I studied during long nights and did my best to remain awake over the best coffee in the world. It's the place where my dreams came to fruition and got crushed just the same.

It's where Jack almost killed me.

Several miles from downtown Seattle lies the spot where Jack hit me that terrible night, leaving me unconscious and on the brink of death. The catalyst for everything that followed.

The only reason I moved to Boston was to find Jack and make him pay for what he did to me.

But Karma has its own way of making things right in life.

Misty—or, as I learned later, Elizabeth Paige was her full legal name—is in jail. Before Jack passed, he confessed he'd tampered with evidence, trying to cover up tax evasion Elizabeth was accused of for her private law firm. It's a federal offense she was hoping to get away with, but she wasn't so lucky.

Jenna is not doing so well. She's gained a ton of weight and is still searching for the one. Though, she's been seen walking around the Boston Common, talking to herself and looking unkempt. She's lost her marbles and can't differentiate reality from fantasy.

I've put our brownstone place on the market, and I plan to sell my catering business and move closer to my family. There's nothing that holds me in Boston anymore. Claire considered buying it, but she changed her mind; she is moving on from catering business and becoming what she has always wanted to be: a pastry chef. The old habits die hard, as they say. Claire and I still text each other every day and exchange daily stories.

Today, I'm visiting with Evelyn—the real Evelyn—Jack's mother, who is mourning Jack's recent death. The day I'd finally confronted him, Jack had stolen my car, and the following day, sat down behind the wheel, drunk, and had a fatal accident on Route 90. The irony isn't lost on me. Poetic justice, if ever I've seen it.

His mother and I meet at a restaurant near Pike Place Market, close to her apartment. I arrive early, soaking in the views and reflecting on how my life has unfolded recently. It's not how I'd envisioned it, but maybe destiny isn't something we build—it's something that builds us.

My thoughts are interrupted when an elderly woman joins my table. She appears fragile, and it's not a surprise, given she is recovering from heart surgery and has recently lost her son. I feel the urge to give her a comforting hug as she looks at me with those big, sorrowful eyes.

"Hi. I'm Evelyn."

I stand up to greet her. "Hi, I'm Emily. It's nice to finally meet you."

We hug, then she steps back to look at me. "You look gorgeous. I can see why Jack fell in love with you."

"Thank you," I say, shyly. As I look at her, I see the resemblance between her and Jack—no doubt this is his actual mother.

Evelyn smiles, though it's a sad, broken thing. We sit down, and for a moment, silence stretches between us, the weight of everything that's happened resting in the space between us.

She clasps her hands together, her fingers trembling. She dives right in, like she's been waiting for this moment all along. "Jack... he wasn't the same after that accident," she says softly, her eyes drifting to the window, as if searching for something far away. "I always knew something had changed in him. He didn't talk about it, but I could see it in his eyes—this guilt he carried with him."

I swallow hard, the memory of the accident flooding back. "He never mentioned it?"

Evelyn shakes her head. "Not once. But a mother knows, you know? I could see it—he was haunted. After he hit that woman and ran, he was never the same. He tried to hide it, but I could feel the darkness in him, eating away at him little by little. It was like a piece of him died that night."

"I hear you."

"The poor woman...Grace Holloway, she could still be alive now, you know?" She looks at me, her eyes etched in guilt as if she's taking the responsibility for someone's death.

I nod slowly. I don't have the courage to tell her that he never killed anyone. The truth can be distorted, and we believe whatever it is we want to believe. But Grace

Holloway is dead. I am Emily now and ready to move on and live my life.

Something unexpected happens, as I cement my decision not to tell her: the anger I once held toward Jack softens into something I can't quite name—maybe pity, maybe sorrow. It's strange to think that, in the end, we were both haunted by the same event, our lives twisted by that single moment of impact on a dark road.

Evelyn's voice pulls me from my thoughts. "I just wish... I could've helped him sooner. I had no idea he had drinking problems. Maybe if I'd known, really known, what was weighing on him—"

I reach across the table, taking her fragile hand in mine. "You did what you could," I say quietly. "None of us could have known how it would end."

She gently squeezes my hand, tears glistening in her eyes. "Thank you for saying that. I hope... wherever he is now, he's found some peace. And the young woman, too. They both deserve peace."

I nod and smile.

As we sit together, the city bustling around us, I realize that I'm finally free—not just from Jack, but from the rage and the need for retribution that has consumed me for so long.

It's over.

And though my path forward is uncertain, it's mine to walk without the weight of the past dragging me down.

I smile at Evelyn, a genuine smile, and for the first time in a long time, I feel light.

The waitress brings our coffee, and we sip in silence. Evelyn gazes at me occasionally, her eyes drifting into the distance. I wonder what she's thinking. Maybe the demise of her estranged son gave her a kind of closure that was hard and easy to accept at the same time. Her lip twitches, and she tries to conceal it by bringing her coffee cup to her lips.

A tear forms at the edge of her eye. She wipes it and looks at me again. "Thank you for visiting me, dear. I hope to see you often."

I nod and give her a small smile. "I have to go now." I stand up and give her a kiss on the right cheek, and she looks pleased. "Take care, Evelyn."

I exit the cafe and walk to the harbor where I used to spend countless days meditating. Evelyn doesn't know she will never see me again. But her sad eyes will stay with me forever.

Yet, I know she is going to be okay.

We both are.

Writing a book is never a solo journey, and I'm endlessly grateful to everyone who made this story possible. To my family and friends, particularly my husband, Chad—thank you for your unwavering support and patience as I disappeared into my writing cave time and time again. Your belief in me has been my anchor.

Thanks to my son, the brightest star in my life, who keeps me laughing and reminds me what life is truly about.

My heartfelt thanks go to my alpha reader and friend, Alison Osborn, who bravely tackled the very first draft. Alison, your support and keen eye have been invaluable, and I'm so grateful for your friendship.

A special thank you to my editor, Jessica Ryn, whose insightful feedback and meticulous attention to detail helped shape this book in ways I couldn't have achieved alone.

Thanks to Adrijus, my talented book cover design guru, who always does an incredible job. To the readers who continue to pick up my books, share them, and connect with these characters—thank you. Your support and love for story-telling keep me going, and I'm so honored to share this journey with you.

Many thanks to the members of the best book group on Facebook—the Psychological Thriller Book Club—and to its admin, Mark Jenkins, who has shown unwavering support for indie authors. The community built in this group is incredible, and I feel fortunate to be among such wonderful authors and readers.

Finally, to every author who has inspired me along the way, thank you for showing me the power of words and the endless possibilities they hold.

ABOUT THE AUTHOR

Nadija Mujagić lives in Massachusetts with her husband, son, and a standard poodle named Koko. In her spare time, she enjoys playing sports and electric bass guitar.

Please follow her on Facebook:

Non Fiction

Ten Thousand Shells and Counting: A Memoir

Immigrated: A Memoir

Fiction

Till a Better World: Woman's Fiction

The Brilliant Mirage: A Thriller

The Exchange: A Psychological Thriller

The Master of Demise: A Psychological Thriller

The Nightmare Under the Mistletoe: A Christmas Thriller Novelette

Lottery Series (Gripping Psychological Thrillers) : 1) Lottery of Secrets

2) Lottery of Lies, 3) Lottery of Revenge

Loretta: A Crime Thriller with Psychological Suspense